CWMTWP
Gossip From the Valleys

David Jandrell

y Lolfa

First impression: 2009

© David Jandrell & Y Lolfa Cyf., 2009

This book is subject to copyright
and may not be reproduced by any means
except for review purposes
without the prior written consent of the publishers.

Cover design: Y Lolfa

ISBN: 9781847710994

Printed on acid-free and partly recycled paper
and published and bound in Wales by
Y Lolfa Cyf., Talybont, Ceredigion SY24 5AP
e-mail ylolfa@ylolfa.com
website www.ylolfa.com
tel 01970 832 304
fax 832 782

1

It is the future. Well into the future. So far into the future, in fact, that the world as you know it is totally unrecognisable. Computers have been obsolete for many decades. Can you imagine a world without computers? Go on then, take some time out to savour the moment...

In the area historically known as South Wales, Nigel, an archaeologist of great renown is involved in one of his biggest projects to date: a dig covering about one and a half square miles. Nigel is an expert on early 22nd century artefacts. He is sure he is close to unearthing the long-lost village of Cwmtwp.

History records that Cwmtwp had been a thriving community until the year 2135, when the government ordered South Wales to be evacuated and flooded to provide a water supply and luxury marina for London, which by this time had expanded as far west as the area once known as Salisbury Plain. London had since been controversially purchased and shipped to America to become a giant museum of 'old tat', while the lake that covered what was once South Wales had become a vast expanse of sludge which was left abandoned by all who lived near it.

As a result of a phenomenon once known as 'Global Warming' but

5

more recently referred to as 'what the hell are we gonna do now?', the sludge level had dropped to such an extent that the area, always regarded as 'a bit on the high side', had become exposed to the elements once again.

The dig had been going fairly well, but there had been no spectacular finds: only the remnants of old buildings, evidence of irrigation systems, Coke cans etc. But Nigel was keen to continue on the basis that you never knew when something strange might turn up.

Then something strange did turn up. Some kids who were messing around on the site found a 'thing'. They hadn't seen anything like it before and gave it to one of the archaeologists just in case it was important. Better still, just in case it was valuable. The archaeologists didn't know what the 'thing' was, and neither did Nigel. He felt it was 'too early' for his field of expertise, more like 21st century, so he passed it onto Bob, a palaeontologist mate of his.

The news had come back that the 'thing' was probably a CD-ROM: a device which was used for storing information. It was quite well preserved in a plastic case, but it was feared that any information it might contain was probably lost forever as something called a 'computer' was required to 'read' the device. As these 'computers' no longer existed, archaeological experts persuaded the Council for Knowledge to fund a team of engineers to try to restart a computer which was housed in the Museum of Gimmickry in New Washington (formerly France). They had managed to get the computer going and all the information had been retrieved. It had been printed and sent to Nigel who now had it in his possession. He opened the package eagerly and read the brief:

Dept of Engineering
University of N Hemisphere
Grand America

Dear Prof N Jones,

Here is the information that was contained on the CD-ROM. It is an archive of a document that was known as a village newsletter. They were produced in the early to mid-21st century, probably by someone who lived in the village and had access to a computer. They gave people information on news and events in their area. This particular archive is from the year 2005. It contains the entire publication of the periodical from that year.

We've read through it and it makes absolutely no sense to us at all. Perhaps you'll have more luck.

Regards,

The Engineering Team

P.S. The newsletter is called 'What's on in Cwmtwp'.

Nigel pressed the letter to his chest and looked up to the skies. A bead of sweat appeared on his brow which he quickly wiped away. "So, I have found Cwmtwp. I was right." He looked at the envelope containing the archive. He started to twitch as if he were frightened to open it. What would he find inside? Would the contents unravel all the mysteries of the past? The secret of the universe? There was only one way to find out. He opened the envelope, pulled out a huge wad of paper and began to read.

 David Jandrell

What's on in *Cwmtwp*

January

Dog Walker Arrested

A Cwmtwp man who was walking his dog was arrested today and taken into custody. Bail was refused pending further enquiries. Sergeant Hogg, boss of Cwmtwp Police Station, said: "I have watched literally hundreds of news reports over the years of murders. I noticed that the body is nearly always found by a man walking his dog and I thought it was about time we had a word with him."

Name Change

A Cwmtwp man has changed his name by deed poll to Mr A. AAAAAAA. "I've always been last in the phone book," he said yesterday, "so I thought I'd change my name so that I'd be the first. Hopefully I'll get a few calls now." Mr A. AAAAAAA, formerly Mr Z. ZZZZZZZ is currently receiving psychiatric help.

Long Sentence

Two local men were today found guilty of stealing a calendar. They were given six months each by the judge at Cwmtwp Crown Court.

Who is He?

A mystery man entered the Spar on Tuesday, bought a pint of milk and left without hanging around the counter and gossiping about other people. He was noticed by a group of women who had been hanging around the shop gossiping about people as they left the shop. The women then hung around the Chemists, the Café and the Butchers and gossiped about him throughout the day, but were unable to identify the stranger. A spokesperson for the women, gossiped: "He just came in the shop, bought a pint of milk and left. He was about average height and had a coat on." NATO has been informed.

Prime Tie for the Rovers

Rumours that Cwmtwp Rovers have drawn Barcelona in the next round of the Cwmtwp and District Cup were today being heralded by local soccer chiefs as a 'cruel hoax'.

Cliché Bound?

A top professor has noticed that people are using clichés too much in every-day conversation. We asked a top English scholar if he agreed. He said, "When all is said and done, and everything's been done and dusted, that's what it boils down to at the end of the day."

Application Turned Down

The application by the committee of the Cwmtwp Lifeboat Association for a licence to organise a raffle and other events to raise funds for a lifeboat has been turned down by the Council on the grounds that Cwmtwp doesn't have a coastline. A spokesman for the Association said, "They're right in a way, we haven't really got a need for one, to be honest."

Slimming Club Closed

Cwmtwp Slimming Club would like to announce that next Thursday's meeting and 'weigh in' has been called off as it coincides with the closing down sale at the cake shop.

Lost Pal Plea

Dai Gullible is desperate to get hold of an old pal, Ron Shady. "I lent him £5,000 two years ago for plastic surgery, and now I don't know what he looks like," Dai said yesterday.

Health and Safety Issue

H&S officials have scuppered Ron Phish's application to patent his latest in-vention – an ejector seat for helicopters. A spokesman for the H&S Executive said today, "We feel that such a device could be very dangerous."

Cup Winners

Cwmtwp Asylum's football team have won the British Asylums Foot-ball Association Cup. In a tight game the psychiatric patients won the match despite being one-nil down at the half-time interval. In the sec-ond half, they won through with two goals in the dying minutes to lift the trophy for the first time in their history. All the goals came from headers.

Bingo Ding Dong!

A fight broke out in the Cwmtwp Bingo club last night when members took offence to two fat ladies who were sitting near the fire escape before the first game started. Mrs Skrote, loudmouth and former captain of the UK Knitting Needle Bending Team, thought that the women had gone along purely to undermine and ridicule the hysterical Bingo Lingo, in particular, the reference to the number 88. The fight was quickly brought under control and the evening continued without any more incidents. Further trouble was averted by Police who intercepted two little ducks which were waddling towards the club and sent them packing.

Pub Act Snubbed

Novac & Goode, a local beat combo, are being ignored by all local pubs. "We just can't get a gig anywhere," said lead singer Norman Novac earlier today. A spokesman for the Licensed Victuallers Association added, "When people ask us what live act is on in the local area, and we say it's Novac and Goode, for some reason they go somewhere else. I can't understand it." Malcolm Goode, paper and comb player with the duo, was said to be utterly distraught about the whole matter.

Town Hall Burnt Down

Cwmtwp Town Hall burnt down this morning due to an electrical fault causing the curtains to catch fire. Built in 1828, the Town Hall will have to be demolished for safety reasons. Ron Hedonist, mayor and general do-gooder, said. "It will be greatly missed as a landmark in the village, as will my great big gaudy necklace which was destroyed in the blaze." The fire brigade were otherwise engaged at the time of the fire, trying to retrieve Mrs Green's hamster from the back of her settee. He is now safely back in his cage.

TV Strife

Edna Glottis has spoken out regarding the situation with her telly viewing. "That's all it is: sport, sport and more sport. It's ridiculous!"

Her husband Bill retorted: "What about Coronation Street, Eastenders, Hollyoaks, Peak Practice, London's Burning, Bad Girls, Crossroads, Where the Heart Is, Casualty, Heartbeat, Emmerdale, Pobol Y Cwm, The Royal, The Bill, Home and Away, Neighbours, Footballers' Wives, Baywatch and Ballykiss-soddin-angel then?"

PhD in Paste

Enid Sprocket, a Cwmtwp woman, has been awarded a PhD from Cwmtwp University. She studied paste for seven years and was today given her cap and gown at the Gasworks Social Club. "It is a great honour to be a world authority on paste," she commented proudly today, "I have certainly put a lot of work into it, and travelled a lot as well. My personal favourites are the Salmon and Beef spreads, they're very tasty. Some of the Eastern European and Asian pastes are a bit bizarre to say the least. Funnily enough, by far the worst I've ever tasted is actually made in this country. It is a crab paste and is only available at the Chemists."

Dog Lover

A Cwmtwp dog owner who was accused of having 'unnatural relationships' with his Alsatian bitch was found guilty of all charges at Cwmtwp Crown Court today. "We are very pleased to get this result," a spokesman for the CwmtwpSPCA said earlier, "it has been a long case and we're glad it's all over." The guilty man was given six months and pick of the litter.

Heavy Metal U-Turn

Leather jacketed, heavily tattooed and long-haired heavy metal fan Don Savage would like to say that Cadmium is now his favourite. "I used to be quite partial to Mercury but I find it a little too runny for my liking these days," he said today.

Martial Arts Beating

Stig Watson, a martial arts expert reputed to be capable of killing with his bare feet, was beaten up by six skinheads outside the chip shop late on Friday night before he had a chance to get his socks off.

Rugby Match Cancelled

Cwmtwp's away game was cancelled on the weekend as a result of their minibus being vandalised outside the Rugby Club on Wednesday night. Mrs Buzzard, who has washed their kit for the last 42 years, posted the team to arrive at the venue because they were unable to arrange alternative transport by Friday morning. The team arrived by second post on Monday by which time it was too late to start the game. A spokesman for the home team said, "It's ridiculous, they know what the post is like these days and she didn't even put a first class stamp on them! They can pay for the bloody sandwiches as well," he added while Dataposting his missus to Sainsbury's.

Songs of Praise in Cwmtwp

The vicar of Cwmtwp would like to pass on the good news that the television people have been in touch with him to ask if they can film an episode of Songs of Praise in the village church. "It was quite a shock to think that they would want to film one of the services at our church. I am looking forward to this very much. For those people wishing to attend, the church is the big building to the north of the village, the one with the big spiky thing sticking out of the top of it."

Police Baffled

Police are baffled as to why Mrs Laura Norder who lives in Letzbee Avenue is not actually in the Police force. "She sounds absolutely perfect for the job," said an absolutely baffled Police spokesman today. Sergeant Hogg, boss of Cwmtwp Police Station was said to be considering looking into the matter.

Mission Postponed

Dai Bond, a Cwmtwp spy, has had to postpone a secret mission to infiltrate the Eastern Bloc and sabotage a plan to take over the free world, as he has got to the final of the darts knockout at the Social club. He will leave for Russia straight after the game.

2

Nigel turned to the next page. It was the start of the 'news' for February 2005. Time for a break and a coffee. As soon as he finished thinking this, a 'ting' from the thought thing told him his coffee was ready. As he picked up his cup, he wondered what the people of 2005 would think if they could see the thought-generated technology he'd just used. He began to wonder how people in 2005 made their coffee, or if they had even had it. He hadn't seen any reference to it in the text he'd read so far. While he was having his break, Nigel thought about lots of other things as well, but they are not relevant here and thus not worth mentioning. Break over, Nigel began to compile his log.

"Open log. January 2005 and nothing seems to have happened in Cwmtwp, nothing much that I can understand anyway. The people talked of things that are unknown to me: the Spar, Bingo, Rugby, a UK Knitting Needle Bending Team, Ballykiss-sodding-angel and much more. What are these? Much of the language is familiar to me, but at this moment I can say that I understand only about 50% of what has been written. I think that the language used may be English, a crude precursor of American, although round about

that time people spoke other languages such as French, Italian and Japanese until the standardisation of pure American. It must have been very confusing for them. I cannot rule out the possibility that this writing is a mixture of all these languages. I will speak to Bob in Palaeontology. Another coffee I think."

'Ting.'

"No, tea this time."

'Ting Ting.'

"Remove last eight seconds from log."

"Reopening log. Bob has told me that geology suggests the Earth suffered a massive tsunami in 2005. He thinks that something of that magnitude would have been noted in documents recording the news. I can see no mention of it here. The Cwmtwp newsletter has cast doubt on the scientific evidence. Perhaps science is wrong; perhaps the tsunami didn't happen. On the other hand, this was January. Perhaps it hadn't happened yet. I must read what happened in February. But first, lunch. I think I'll have ham, chips and peas."

'Ting, Ding, Squidge.'

"No, chicken curry and chips."

'Ping, Squibble, Squooble.'

"And coffee."

'Ting.'

What's on in *Cwmtwp*

February

New Restaurant Opens

O'Twatterly's, a new Irish theme restaurant, opened its doors to a select few last night prior to the official opening next Thursday. We went along and sampled a few of the dishes prepared especially for the evening by head chef Sean McFilth, who washed his hands for the occasion. Highly recommended is the Irish mixed grill, which consists of roast potatoes, boiled potatoes, mashed potatoes and chips. Seamus O'Twatterly, the owner, has suggested that people book early for the opening night and has pointed out that the restaurant will be closed for lunch every day between 1 and 2pm.

Terrorist Apprehended

A supposed terrorist was stopped going through passport control at Cwmtwp Airport on Saturday afternoon. He was immediately beaten up by Police who then handed him over to a scientist, who gave him some of that stuff that makes you tell the truth. It has emerged that he was on a mission to make an assault on Cwmtwp Zoo and hold out until all the ostriches had been released.

Society Criticised

The Cwmtwp Society of Lovers of Acronyms has been severely criticised by Sergeant Hogg, boss of Cwmtwp Police Station, because the first letters of their organisation do not spell out a word. "This is just not on!" Sgt Hogg retorted from the station canteen earlier today.

Pop Taken Off-Sale at Panto

The drink 7-Up has been taken off sale at Cwmtwp Playhouse for the duration of the Panto Season. This is as a result of smutty comments shouted from the audience during the first show last Monday regarding Snow White's preferences. Peter Tallboy, who plays Sleepy said today, "The comments were in very bad taste, but a cracking idea nonetheless."

15

UFO Sighted

Reports of a UFO sighting over the village was neither confirmed nor denied by the relevant authority today. "We can neither confirm nor deny this report as it hasn't been reported to us," said a spokesman from the relevant authority. He went on: "And having seen some issues of their newsletter in the past, God only knows who they would have reported it to!"

Milk Marketing Board Announcement

A spokesman today said, "It was us!

Cwmtwp Band's First Single

The Plebbs, a very secretive Cwmtwp band, will release their first single next week. They try to keep their identities secret, but we can reveal their names as our reporter secretly filmed them at their gig at The Cwmcarnegie Hall last week. They are: Ludwig on the drums, Roland on the organ and Gibson on the guitar. We hope that the two ballads on their record will do well. They are entitled 'I Love You' on the front side and 'Kiss Me' on the backside.

Missing Brush

A Cwmtwp road sweeper called the Police at 7.17am yesterday to report that his brush had been stolen. Police arrived on the scene to find the distraught man trying to scoop up litter using a Microwave Chips box that he had found in the street. The Police cordoned off the area and the scenes of crime officer was called, together with forensic scientists. People on their way to work were questioned and the postman was put into custody along with the milkman as joint 'prime suspects'. The road sweeper said: "I put my brush down to run after a plastic bag that was blowing around and when I came back… hang on a minute, it's over by there."

Record Till Takings

The village hall bar has announced pre-tax profits of £24,567.78 for the last quarter. The caretaker of the hall said, "This is quite a staggering amount to have taken in such a short time and for such a small bar." He later added, "It is also quite sad when you bear in mind that the room is only used by Cwmtwp Alcoholics Anonymous and they only meet on the third Monday of every month."

Clairvoyance Works!

We rang Mystic Mwfanwy this morning and she said, "Of course it does!" Then we asked her if clairvoyance really works.

Name Change

Miss Alice Cooper of Cwmtwp has applied to Somerset House to change her name as she is fed up with references to 'Schools Out' wherever she goes. "My parents are of the sixties era," she said yesterday, "and they decided to name us kids after their favourite rock stars. The trouble is, they didn't think of the consequences thirty years later."

Miss Cooper added, "I hope I can get it changed fairly quickly as I'm at my wits end." Her three brothers Emerson, Lake and Palmer were unavailable for comment at their home yesterday.

Thesaurus Accident

A very large Thesaurus fell from the top shelf at the Library and landed on the head of a man who was walking down the aisle at the time, knocking him out. Our reporter went to visit him at his home and said that the victim had commented that he was, "Not bad, been better, so-so, okay, fair to middling, bearing up, all right, mediocre… "

Maestro Moves On

The leader and conductor of the Cwmtwp Philharmonic Orchestra has moved from the village to take up residence in New York. He will still lead the orchestra, but will travel to each venue from the USA and meet up with the musicians prior to the concerts. We asked him if his move was down to trying to fulfil his spiritual side and to transpose the ethnic diversity of the city into his music. He replied, "Call me a fuddy-duddy, but the New Yorkers tend not to refer to me as 'Dai the Baton'."

Two Companies Merge

BOLL (Banquets of Luxurious Lusciousness) and former competitors OCKS (Outstanding Culinary Knockout Spreads) have decided to pool their resources and become one company providing corporate lunches for big business do's in Cwmtwp Conference Centre. To avoid confusion, they have decided to keep their original name 'tags' and amalgamate them into a new company name rather than make up a new one.

From now on they will be known as "OCKSBOLL" as a result of a small matter brought to the attention of the Board by a printer who had been hired to produce the new company's stationery.

Bank Robber's Description

A bank robber who got away with £4.2 million from Cwmtwp Bank was described as being 'very rich' by the Bank Manager earlier today. Sergeant Hogg, boss of Cwmtwp Police Station, was said to be on the lookout for him. We caught up with Sergeant Hogg in the chip shop and he had to admit that he had not had a sighting of the robber, but would check the cake shop, "Just in case he was in there."

Mixed Fortunes at Gallery

Disaster struck at Cwmtwp Art Gallery on Wednesday morning. Vera and Nancy, cleaners at the Gallery, opened up to find a half-eaten pasty and a portion of chips wrapped in newspaper on the floor near the fire exit. They cleared up the discarded items and swept the rest of the room, only to find that they had thrown away a modern art display worth countless thousands of pounds! The Gallery saved some face later in the day when an eccentric American multi-millionaire art collector paid £1.2 million for some orange peel, six pips and a Toffee Crisp wrapper which had been left in an ashtray near the checkout in the Gallery's canteen.

Double World Champ

Ron Myopia, the most short-sighted bloke in Cwmtwp, bought 250 tubes of Savlon as a job lot believing them to be tubes of toothpaste. After three years of brushing with the Savlon, he won both the 'World's Filthiest Teeth' and 'World's Healthiest Gums' Championships at the British Dental Awards in London last Tuesday.

Astronomy Find Poo-pooed

A previously unknown Nebula which was discovered by Cwmtwp amateur astronomer Dai Galileo caused a brief ripple of interest through the scientific world last week. However, the Nebula was identified as pigeon shit on the lens of Dai's telescope by proper astronomers yesterday.

Bus Dispute Hots Up

A bitter row between two bus companies operating the same Cwmtwp to Cardiff route boiled over on the weekend in a fare-cutting price war. The Omnibusman has been called in the settle the dispute.

Enquiry into Darts Fight

The committee of Cwmtwp Darts Club was called into an emergency session today following an incident when two members started fighting during a big league game.

They decided to ban whichever member had started the fracas, but found that no members who were in the room at the time were prepared to come forward with any details. One person did issue a statement. Bill Tungsten-Shaft, the team captain, said, "As far as I could make out, it was double three of one and half a double six of the other."

Tortoise Man Treatment

Reg Carapace, a Cwmtwp man with a personality disorder, has been referred to a top psychiatrist who specialises in dual personalities and confidence problems. Reg's wife, Freda, spoke of her relief at the fact that her husband was finally getting his ongoing delusion addressed by an expert. "Reg started thinking he was a tortoise about five years ago. He's been to several doctors with no joy, but this guy came highly recommended. If anyone can get Reg to come out of his shell, he can."

Big Money Golf Challenge

Ron Trudgey, Cwmtwp's World Blind Golf Champion, has challenged Simon Ping-Replica the sighted club Pro to a game over nine holes at Cwmtwp Golf Club for a prize purse of £5,000. To ensure that both players start off on an even keel, the match will tee-off at midnight on Thursday.

New Column Next Week

From next week onwards we will feature a new column where you can put questions to our resident expert Dai. If you have any questions at all, address your query to 'Ask Dai' at our offices and he will sort them out for you.

3

Nigel sat back in his chair and raised his eyes to the heavens. He took a deep breath and blew it out through pursed lips. What does all this mean? In two whole months there had been no mention of any world shattering news stories! Were there not any to report? Was 2005 very quiet?

He had noticed a reference to another new word: 'music' – and had asked fellow academics if they had an inkling of what this word meant. He was very excited to receive this incoming message:

> "Nigel. Music, as far as we know, was used as a form of audible entertainment. People listened to 'sounds' and 'noises' that when placed in conjunction with each other produced music. It had a 'beat' and sometimes people joined in, using their voices to complement the final product. When they did this, it was known as 'singing'. Presumably, people who did singing were known as 'singists', although we have no documented references to 'singists' so their contribution to music must not have been regarded as all that important.

> "The phenomenon of music died out, although it is not

known when, due to it being made illegal in an attempt to eradicate the number of lawsuits that were rife at the time. Music was made up of a series of tones, or notes as they were called. As there were a limited number of these to use, a point was reached whereby all combinations had been used and 'tunes' began to reappear. Mathematics showed that no more original tunes could be made from these notes and lawsuits claiming that people had stolen 'their' tunes became so widespread, the governments of the day decided to ban it. Hope this helps."

Nigel was pleased that one of his academic friends could shed some light on this new word. But what about these: Omnibusman? Toothpaste? Emerson, Lake and Palmer? The British Dental Awards? Ocksboll? Toffee Crisp wrapper? Was there anyone, anywhere, that could pass comment on these? Nigel seriously doubted it.

He thought about it for a while but the thought thing was silent. It obviously had serious doubts as well. Then he thought about a ham sandwich.

'Bing Bong.'
And one appeared.

What's on in *Cwmtwp*

March

Cwmtwp Metro Under Fire

Transport trouble-shooter Sir Jones Harvey-John has branded Cwmtwp Underground Railway system a classic example of 'utter madness'. Following a study of the failing service, it was discovered that the tracks were only a foot longer than the village itself, there was only one station and the 'passengers' had to walk up and down steps which totalled 4.3 miles to access the platform.

"We thought we'd utilise the existing tunnels left after the demise of the mining industry in order to save a few bob," said Dai Loco, owner of the service, "but we think that it may be a bit 'deep' for most people's liking." Sir Jones added: "People object to paying £5 to get on a train and then get straight off it on the other side just to end up in the same place." Hilda Thicke, a regular passenger for nine years, said, "I think it's great!"

Toilet Doors Extended

The doors in Cwmtwp public toilets are to be lengthened so that they reach the floor due to complaints from users regarding local limbo dancers who frequent the premises for voyeuristic purposes.

Can't Help

Hilda Thicke has contacted the Welsh FA asking to be put in touch with two referees to speak up for her on a job application form that she is filling in. A spokesman from the WFA said, "How can any of our refs put a good word in for this woman? We don't even know her!"

Ask Dai

Bill Troutly of Cwmtwp has the honour of sending in the first question for our resident expert. Bill, a retired schoolboy, asks: "Dai, in the pub there is a sign by the till saying 'All notes tendered at the bar will be checked using a counterfeit detector'. Do you think this is a good idea?"

DAI SAYS: "I think they'd be a lot better off if they used a real detector, Bill."

Lonely Hearts *Pick 'm' Up*

☉☉NEW COLUMN☉☉

23 year old MALE, good looking, fit, with high sex drive, seeks very old, very rich, terminally ill woman for a short-term marriage and long-term inheritance.
Contact: Box 001

I'm a fit MALE, 41 years old. Millionaire, own car, yacht, cottage in Brittany, detached mansion with heated indoor and outdoor swimming pools, tennis court and stables. Impressed?
Contact: Don't bother, I just thought I'd let you know what a lot I've got.

Interested in solvents? I am! If you enjoy 'having a good time' in vats of highly volatile solvents, get in touch now! Must be non-smoker.
Contact: Box 002

Bendix washing machine for sale. Can be seen working. Buyer collects. £150 ono.
Contact: Box 003

The Anti-Procrastination Club are looking for female companions for their annual trip to Blackpool. We are looking for good, clean, 'no strings attached' hanky panky with no questions asked. No time wasters please.
Contact: Box 004

Cricket Suspicion not Proved

Suspicions that cricket is the most boring thing in the world prompted us into partaking in a fact-finding exercise. We sent a reporter along to a cricket match to see if the extent of tedium associated with the game is as bad as suspected. Unfortunately, our survey has proved inconclusive. On his way to the match, our reporter bumped into some blokes who were on their way to watch some paint dry. He decided that going with them was a much better option.

Ant Safety Fears

Residents are being warned to keep any pet ants safely indoors until Mrs Tompkinson's aardvark which escaped on Thursday is safely back under lock and key in the shed.

Snooker Champ Nickname

Mark Skidd, Cwmtwp snooker champion, has been given the nickname 'the Tornado' by fellow players. They decided to use this metaphor in line with other players such as 'the Whirlwind' and 'the Hurricane'. 'The Tornado' nickname came about as a result of the massive bouts of flatulence he displays every time he bends over the table to play a shot.

Church Roof to be Repaired

The vicar has announced that the parishioners have raised enough money to have the church roof fixed and to have some other jobs done. At the Parochial Church Council meeting today he said, "We've been holding jumble sales, flea markets and 'guess the weight of the cake' competitions over the last ten years and have amassed the amount of £5.42. Then, six months ago we put a swear-box into the Sunday School and as a result we can now get the roof fixed, have a conservatory put on the back, buy a heated font and Jacuzzi, a new Wurlitzer organ with digital sequencer and polyphonic synth and a solid gold collection plate."

The verger issued a statement which we cannot print, but it intimated that he was pleased with the success of the swear-box and it also raised enough cash for a new pulpit.

Snow White Cover Blown

Snow White look-alike Emma Cardboard has spent a lifetime trying to shake off unwanted references to the Disney character. "I actually do look a lot like Snow White and over the years I've just got fed up with people making comments about '7-Up' and other lewd dwarf-related innuendos," she said. Her efforts took a backward step on Saturday as she expressed her disappointment in the chemists when her photos still hadn't come back. When given the news that the firm that develops film for the shop were late with their deliveries, Emma was heard to say, "One day my prints will come."

Ask Dai

Tim Stiltskin of Cwmtwp asks. "Dai, can you settle an argument between me and my missus? I reckon that there's five different types of people and she reckons there's six. What is the answer Dai?"

DAI SAYS: "There's only three types of people Tim: those that can count and those that can't."

Mystery Object Causes Concern

A mystery object handed in to Cwmtwp Museum was still causing concern yesterday, according to our sources at the museum. The unidentified mystery object has been examined by all the experts at the museum but the exact nature of the object still remains a mystery. We spoke to the curator of the museum this morning and asked if he could comment on what the mystery object could be. The curator was able to issue the following statement: "The term 'mystery object' should give you a very big clue as to our conclusions as to what the object may be. As we have not yet been able to identify the object, we are still referring to it as the 'mystery object' until such time that we can put a name to it. It has been suggested that it may be a 'thing', and currently that theory is being investigated."

Unusual Delivery at Florists

Cwmtwp Florists have taken a special delivery of Triffids for Bob Fretless-Bass. He ordered them for his wife who has run off with the milkman. "I got the idea from the 'Say it with flowers' poster in the shop," he said today. "Let's hope the old cow gets the message."

Rovers Seeking Keeper

Ron Sprig, manager of Cwmtwp Rovers, has appealed to anyone with goal-keeping experience to turn out for the side's game against the Slaughterhouse XI on Saturday. The appeal follows the news that their regular goalie, Dai Sailor, has been involved in a road accident. Eye-witnesses spoke of an incident in the village on Tuesday when Dai crossed the road and a double-decker bus went under him.

Doubt Cast on Drowning Theory

What seemed to be a simple case of drowning has taken a sinister twist in the circumstances leading up to the death of a brewery worker at Cwmtwp Brewery. Colleagues came in to work on Monday morning to find the body floating in a vat of pale ale and Police were satisfied that he had fallen in and drowned over the weekend. Security guards discovered a flaw in the theory when they watched the security video that covered events in the factory over the weekend. "It is apparent that the worker fell into the vat," said the head of Security, "but his death is a mystery to us as it is clear from watching the tape that he actually managed to get out four times to have a pee."

Wrong Career Move?

Tony Blare, a former Cwmtwp rat catcher, has had to abandon his new career as a 'look-alike' of the former Prime Minister. An agent who was approached by Mr Blare said that the whole idea of professional look-alikes was that the look-alikes looked like the person they were supposed to look like. Granted, his name was very, very similar to the former PM's, but Mr Blare bore absolutely no resemblance whatsoever to the real Mr Blair. Today, Mr Blare was pleading with his ex-boss to give him his old job back, so far without success.

Patent Application

Bob Silage, a local hill farmer, has contacted the Patent Office to put forward his discovery that there are two new things that sheep can be used for: meat and wool.

Hard Luck Sir Roger

Sir Roger Rhys Jones Williams Morgan Griffiths Smythe Ponsonby Barrington Rathbone St John Speedwagon Mastercard Lewis Bicarbonate Brasenose Eel Envelope Ullricht Benson Squidgelin Les Abacus Francis Angelis Peterstone Robinson Rutle Gilmour Inkjet Walmar Dennis Tilsley Highland Spring Arcade Embassy Jenkins, the man with the longest name in the village, hired this column to make an announcement but we ran out of room before we got to it.

4

Nigel pondered the articles that he had read so far.

"Open log. I am still none the wiser. I have read about the events in Cwmtwp from January, February and March 2005 and things don't seem to make sense. I have noticed that there appear to be some very prominent characters who were active in Cwmtwp at this time: Hilda Thicke, Sergeant Hogg and Dai. Let's deal with Hilda Thicke first. "History tells me that the 'Hilda' tag was used for females, but who was she? Perhaps a fountain of knowledge and wisdom. She is mentioned in the newsletter a lot. Maybe a great scholar of her day. A pillar of the establishment? Well respected? I hope that I will read more about this Hilda Thicke.

"As far as Sergeant Hogg is concerned, the only thing I know about him at the moment is that he was the 'boss of Cwmtwp Police Station'. It is well documented that there were people known as 'Police' who enforced the law in those days and it is certain that Sergeant Hogg was one of these.

I have also found references to the word 'hog' in ancient scripts. The linguists tell me that hogs were slovenly beasts who ate continuously and were despised by many humans of the day. However, the difference in spelling between hog and Hogg suggests that they are unconnected and it would be unfair of me to suggest otherwise.

"Lastly, Dai. I have come to the conclusion that Dai is a tag for a male. My reason for this is that we know there was a very prominent female active in the 20th century called Lady Di. I am assuming that the addition of 'a' changes the gender of the tag to male. I have nothing to support this theory other than a strong gut feeling. For the purposes of this log, I will refer to Dai as a male unless I discover otherwise.

"Dai seems to be a person of great knowledge and integrity. People look up to him. They ask his advice and respect his views. I am confident that I will glean much more information from him and thus be able to form a very accurate picture of what life was like in 2005. If my assumptions about Hilda Thicke are correct, Dai could be her intellectual equal. Were they prophets of their time? Oracles? The only way I can find out is to read on. But first, a game of table-tennis."

'Ping Pong.'

Yes, the thought thing also provided leisure activities. During his game, Nigel wondered if he would ever find out what Sir Roger Rhys Jones Williams Morgan Griffiths Smythe Ponsonby Barrington Rathbone St John Speedwagon Mastercard Lewis Bicarbonate Brasenose Eel Envelope Ullricht Benson Squidgelin Les Abacus Francis Angelis Peterstone Robinson Rutle Gilmour Inkjet Walmar Dennis Tilsley Highland Spring Arcade Embassy Jenkins had to say.

What's on in *Cwmtwp*

April

Punctuation Arrest

Malcolm Prattling, a Cwmtwp ring wormer, has been arrested by a crack 'punctuation squad' on a charge of being 'very sparse' with punctuation in his written work. "It's as if punctuation didn't exist in Mr Prattling's eyes," said Sergeant Hogg, boss of Cwmtwp Police Station this morning. Mrs Prattling was said to be very concerned and made a brief statement earlier: "It is true that Malcolm doesn't care too much for punctuation, but I hope the courts will be lenient and give him the shortest sentence allowable under the law."

Hilda Slated

Hilda Thicke was slated by fellow mourners and the vicar when it was noticed that she had 'laughed out loud' all the way through a funeral held at Cwmtwp Church last Tuesday. However, sighs of relief were heard when Hilda explained that she had just 'got' a joke she had heard in the Social Club three weeks earlier.

New Column Scrapped

As a result of the massive influx of inappropriate ads coming into our office over the last week, we have decided to discontinue the Lonely Hearts column. Our editor said, "I am absolutely disgusted with the suggestions that some people have wanted printed." He added that he was "fixed up" for the foreseeable future.

Grand Prix Mix-Up

A group of local lads hired as pit-stop hands for the Cwmtwp Grand Prix were sacked by Ferrari after their first pit-stop. They removed the wheels in a record three seconds, but made off with them to the car boot sale at the pub and sold them for a fiver each – sadly for them, to Sergeant Hogg, boss of Cwmtwp Police Station.

David Jandrell

Ruled Out of Olympics

Roger Over-Cautious has been in touch with the Olympic Committee to rule himself out of the next games. Today he explained his decision. "I bought some cream from the Chemist's to put on a gnat bite and I noticed that it contained steroids. I don't play any sports, but I thought I'd let them know just in case they picked me to do something in the next games. It'll save any embarrassment should I win a gold and have to be stripped of my title as a result of drug testing. I'm sure they will understand." Roger is 42 and seriously insane.

Cold Spell Looming

The first sign of a cold spell reared its head on Saturday when a brass monkey called into Cwmtwp garage and enquired as to whether they did small welding jobs.

Sorry Dolores!!

We have printed this free of charge to serve as an apology to Dolores Tarte of Cwmtwp, following a mistake we made in the last issue. She says: "Last week, the 'What's on in Cwmtwp' newsletter printed my ad in the wrong column. The ad to sell my washing machine was printed in the Lonely Hearts column by mistake. The washing machine is still for sale if anyone is interested. If you fancy a 'good time' see my message in last week's small ads column, or meet me in the bus shelter after 'shut tap' on Saturday night."

Not as Serious as Expected

Howard Pendragon was admitted to Cwmtwp Royal Infirmary on Tuesday morning with what was at first thought to be a serious medical problem. Howard himself takes up the story: "I was cycling to work when I noticed my legs suddenly becoming very warm. I looked and they had swelled up quite a lot. As there is a history of legs in our family and I was near the hospital, I thought I'd better pop in and get them checked out." After a brief examination and the removal of Howard's bicycle clips, the medical emergency was found to be nothing more serious than a rather violent bout of diarrhoea.

Announcement: Bash at Snuffy's

Snuffy, Cwmtwp's vampire slayer, is having a barbecue on Saturday. All invited – guests limited to 24.

Ask Dai

Little Timmy Tonkin from Cwmtwp Junior School asks this week's question. "Dai, can you help me with my homework? Our teacher told us to find out why you can't look directly at the sun during a solar eclipse."

DAI SAYS: "Simple Timmy. That's because the moon will be in the way."

Jenny Clodhopper aged 13 of Cwmtwp asks: "Dai, can you help me with my homework? I have to compare and contrast Thomas Hardy and Geoffrey Chaucer. I don't know where to start!"

DAI SAYS: "Easy Jenny, they both made films with Stan Laurel, except for Geoffrey Chaucer."

Divorce Announced

Edna and Harry Auld, believed to be the longest-married couple in Cwmtwp, have announced their intention to divorce, three days after their 133rd wedding anniversary. Harry, 151 and Edna, 149 said that they were to divorce after 130 miserable years of marriage. "We hated each other from our third year together," said Edna today. Harry said, "It will be a good thing when the divorce comes through. Perhaps we can start again and map out new lives while we still have the chance." We asked Edna why they had decided to leave it so long before divorcing. "Well, we thought we'd wait till the kids died," she said.

Cheating Man Apprehended

A Cwmtwp man who was caught climbing over the wall at Cwmtwp Rovers' ground on Saturday was ticked off by Police who told him to wait until the end of the game and leave the ground through the main gates like any normal person.

Unusual Gig for Gloria

Gloria Tarte, a Cwmtwp stripper and exotic dancer, did a very strange gig last weekend at Cwmtwp Nudist Colony. "I was very surprised when I got the booking," she said earlier today from her boudoir. "I've done some strange shows in the past, but this one takes the biscuit. They asked me to go on stage naked and when the curtain drew back, all I heard was, 'Cor, go on luv, get 'em on!'"

Offensive Sign to Go

Visitors and patients at Cwmtwp Infirmary have complained to the Hospital Board about a sign in the main building. "There are signs everywhere saying things like 'X-Ray left', 'Casualty right' and 'Wards straight on' that are essential in a place like that," said a visitor yesterday, "but I really do object to the one that says 'Psychiatry round the bend'. It is offensive!" Hilda Thicke, the Psychiatric ward's best customer for the last decade, said, "I can't see anything wrong with it."

Man Found Sane After All

A Cwmtwp man whose sanity has been in question for a number of years was today found sane by a panel of psychiatrists after undergoing a series of tests. When shown a set of cards with blotches on them and asked if they reminded him of anything, he said that they reminded him of a Rorschach Inkblot Test.

Memorial Statue Slated

Shrieks of horror from local dignitaries greeted the unveiling of a sculpture commissioned to commemorate the service of outgoing Cwmtwp Mayor Bert Heathen at the Square yesterday. A spokesman for the Council said, "We think that the sculptor may have misinterpreted our request for a 'bust'. We assumed that he would have produced a 'head and shoulders' sculpture but it is plain to see that he has actually produced the other sort of 'bust' which has caused a great deal of embarrassment." Bert's wife, Gloria, was said to be distraught at the nature of the statue and will take steps to have the offending memorial removed. Phil Habitat, beaten finalist for Bert's Mayoral position, issued a statement saying, "Well, you've only got to look at Gloria to realise it is very apt!"

According to the word on the street, most villagers agree with Phil and believe that the statue should stay.

Hilda in Guinness Book

Hilda Thicke has been in touch with us to say that she has an entry in the Guinness Book of Records. We sent an excited reporter to her home to check out the claim and inform us as to the nature of her 'achievement'. Dai Bookand-pencil, our reporter, was able to tell us that the entry read, 'Happy Birthday Hilda from Vern'.

Hogg in Trouble

Sergeant Hogg, boss of Cwmtwp Police Station, has received a warning from Police chiefs following an embarrassing incident in which he bought four stolen alloys from a car boot sale. After investigating the matter fully it was decided that he had acted in good faith and did not know the wheels had been stolen. He got off with a sound ticking-off from his superiors. We asked if Hogg would like to make a statement but he was unavailable for comment. According to a spokesman for the Police, Hogg was presently 'scouring the menu at the Chinese take-away, in pursuit of some instant comfort'.

New Word Proposed

Alex Icon, a Cwmtwp wordsmith, is trying to get a new word introduced into the English Language. "I coined the word whilst playing 'Scrabble' last week; in fact I won the game with it," he said excitedly from his study. "It's probably the longest word in the language that contains only one letter appearing 11 times consecutively." The word 'NNNNNNNNNN' is said to mean 'constipation'. The Oxford English Dictionary and Call my Bluff have been informed.

Swearing Club Announcement

Bill Cussworthy, chairman of Cwmtwp Swearing Club, has issued this statement giving details of their AGM and post-meeting eats and drinks: "****, ****** and ***** **** in the **** at 7.30 ****. Please **** ******* by the ******* and ******* **** *******." We reserved the right to censor the statement for legal reasons. We hope if anyone does turn up, it'll be a good night.

Cure for insomnia?

A computer buff was brought in to discuss recent developments in IT to a chronic insomnia sufferer. After only two hours, the treatment worked.

Hogg in the Doghouse

Sergeant Hogg, boss of Cwmtwp Police Station, was given a good talking to by Police Chiefs on Friday. A spokesman from the Police Complaints Commission said of the incident, "Sergeant Hogg had been following a vehicle for a number of miles and suspected that it was carrying an unsafe load. He pulled the vehicle over and told the driver that he was losing his load, booked him for the offence and made the driver sweep the 'mess' up. We then got a telephone call from Cwmtwp Council Offices which informed us that the vehicle in question had been gritting the road at the time."

Suspicious Vehicle

A suspicious vehicle left in Stratt Street three weeks ago which has not been moved since was identified as a 'skip' by council officials today.

Vampire Alert!

Suspicions that vampire activity may be imminent were raised today when Snuffy, Cwmtwp's 'vampire slayer' ordered two dozen garlic steaks from the butchers.

5

Nigel was very intrigued by one article in the April 2005 archive which included what could prove to be the earliest known reference to the Olympic Games! If verified as such, Nigel could be thrust into the highest echelons of academia.

"Open log. I believe I have strong evidence that the Olympic Games existed as early as 2005. I am not sure, however, that the Games took the same format then as they do today. Nowadays, of course, the Games are contested between pharmaceutical companies to see who can produce the best performance-enhancing drugs. In 2005, I believe people actually participated in the Games and took the drugs themselves! The Games are much safer now of course. The drugs are introduced into machines to analyse their strength in order to ascertain the winner. No people are involved. I'm not sure, but I think that in those days the participants may have had to undergo some sort of physical activity in order to choose the winner, perish the thought. Still, it's nice to see that the whole ethos behind the Games – finding a winner –

has remained unchanged all this time.

"I am pleased to note that Hilda Thicke, Dai and Sergeant Hogg are still very prominent in the newsletter and I am monitoring their progress as I read on. Still no great words of wisdom from them, but I am hoping that they will shed some light on some of the mysteries of the day.

"I have also made an interesting discovery: I thought about a cup of coffee earlier on and nothing happened. The thought thing is obviously not working properly. I'll have to think about getting it fixed."

'Ting.'

A coffee appeared!

"I have made another interesting discovery. If you think about getting the thought thing fixed, it fixes itself. Good innit? Close log."

Hogg Sorts it Out

Sergeant Hogg, boss of Cwmtwp Police Station, was called to Cwmtwp Electrical Store today to sort out a minor fracas. Irate customer Bill Festival-Hall takes up the story. "I took my TV back because I thought there was something wrong with it. It only seems to pick up soaps! The man in the shop said that it was not possible for TVs to just pick up soaps so I challenged him to turn it on in the shop in front of me. I was gob smacked! Instead of Coronation Street there was a series about flowers on. I just couldn't understand it!" Sergeant Hogg solved the problem when he spoke to Mrs Festival-Hall and she admitted taping soaps and playing them back when there was no soap on any channel. "That put a stop to her little game!" Sergeant Hogg added smugly from the front of the queue at the fast-food van earlier on.

Rugby Fans Up in Arms!

Plans to end the age-old tradition of swapping shirts at the end of Cwmtwp Ladies' Rugby matches have been blasted as grossly unfair by the 500 or so men who wear long Macs and arrive at the ground about three minutes before the end of their games.

Floral Pet Name Exposed

Brenda Neighbour told us today of a 'pet name' she has coined for her hubby Bill. "I decided to name my old man after that Swiss flower that Julie Andrews sang about in The Sound of Music because he's an Idle-swine."

Ask Dai

In recognition of British Surrealism Week, Dai has tackled a question from the Chairman of the Cwmtwp Surrealists Association, Phil Staple who asks, "Dai, what is the difference between a duck?"

DAI REPLIES: "That's an easy one Phil: the other leg's both the same."

Foot Odour Sufferer Referred

A Cwmtwp man suffering from chronic foot odour has been referred to a specialist following complications caused as a result of advice given to him by his GP. Initially, the GP advised the man to put on a clean pair of socks every day as he felt that this may reduce the noxious fumes that exuded from his feet. After three weeks of following the instructions to the letter, the man, Mr Vern Thicke, now finds it impossible to get his boots on. When he told his GP of the problem, he was immediately referred to a specialist for an emergency consultation. The consultant's report is eagerly awaited by all.

Stereo Too Loud?

Mike Pardon has been showing off his new stereo to a few chosen members of the locality. Our reporter Timmy Papers went to listen to it yesterday and told us, "It was mad. My ears are still buzzing. When I commented on how loud it was, he said he had it on twice as loud when he was on his own. Well, all I can say is I'm glad I'm never with him when he's on his own!"

Astronaut Criticised

Cwmtwp astronaut, Buzz Collins was criticized by officials at Cwmtwp Dole Office yesterday. A spokesman for the Dole Office said, "Buzz spent seven years in America training to be an astronaut. He qualified last week, flew over to the UK and came into our office to sign on this morning. The trouble is, he registered as an astronaut which is what he is, but added that he wasn't prepared to travel. I don't reckon he wants to work!"

Close Shave for Dennis

Dennis Torchminder, a retired pit worker from the village, has nearly won the lottery for the 200th week on the trot it was announced today. "I've won a few tenners and once I had four numbers, but last week was the closest I ever came to the big one. The bloke next door won it," he said earlier.

Kidnappers Still at Large

The kidnapping of Tommy Bratte, Cwmtwp's most annoying child was nearly solved today when his abductors sent him home with the ransom note. Police said that the lad was still missing after his parents sent him back with the money.

Countdown Champ Unhappy

Bill Braine, Cwmtwp's recent Countdown Champion returned to the village today after winning the prestigious TV word quiz. We sent a photographer round to take a few snaps of Bill and his prize, a brand new dictionary. After the photo session, Bill made a quick statement: "I'm very disappointed with the prize to be honest. Let's face it, I've just won Countdown – what the hell do I want a dictionary for?"

New Shampoo on the Market

Buzz Collins, Cwmtwp astronaut and celeb has 'launched' a brand of shampoo aimed at the male end of the market. The newest product is designed specially for astronauts and is called 'Wash and Boldly Go.' A spokesman for Captain Picard said that he would endorse the product but added that he wouldn't use it himself. He did not give any explanation for why this was the case.

Chapter's Dilemma

Butch Grebbler, the leader and hardest of the Cwmtwp Hell's Angels Chapter, has been displaying his new leather jacket. He spent months and hundreds of pounds decorating it with appropriate logos and Hell's Angels-type scenes. The centrepiece of the jacket is a huge embroidered slogan 'Cwmtwp Hell's Angles'. Brian Slime, second-in-command of the Chapter said, "You can tell him if you want to, I'm not!"

Snake Carrier

Ron Bank-Rupt, whose Cwmtwp Sports Shop went out of business, has approached the Snake Club of Great Britain in an attempt to supply Snake Carrying Cases to its members. "I had a lot of cue cases left in the shop when it closed down and I had no idea what to do with them. Then I thought they'd make ideal cases for people with snakes who may like to take them out now and again." The chairman of the Snake Club was said to be considering the offer and would get back to Ron when hell froze over.

Opposition to Twinning

Plans to 'twin' Cwmtwp with the village of Khaakk, a run-down hole in the ground in Afghanistan, have been vehemently opposed by the residents. The disgruntled mayor of Khaakk, Mustapha Washe, said, "All three residents and all the goats are up in arms. We will oppose this move to the hilt." Cwmtwp Council officials were planning a fact-finding trip to Khaakk, stopping off at Miami on the way, to negotiate with Khaakk officials.

 David Jandrell

University Challenge Flop

The team from Cwmtwp University were laughed off screen on last night's edition of University Challenge only two minutes after the start of the programme. The derision began immediately following the team's introductions. "It wasn't their names that caused the hilarity," said the quiz-master, "it was the fact that they all said they were 'reading writing' that did it."

Strange Letter Found

A Cwmtwp postman has reported a strange letter that was posted in Cwmtwp pillar box. "I've never seen anything like it in my life," he said today in a state of shock. The letter which was addressed to The Times newspaper contained a completed Times crossword.

Sergeant Hogg, boss of Cwmtwp Police Station said, "This has obviously been posted by someone passing through the village. I wouldn't get excited over it, it's probably just a one-off."

Woman Found Sane

A woman who wasted a whole week watching EastEnders, Coronation Street, Emmerdale Farm, The Bill, Heartbeat, Merseybeat, Judge John Deed, Midsomer Murders, Bad Girls, London's Burning and Casualty was today pronounced normal by a female psychiatrist.

Vern Finally out of the Closet

Shrieks of horror greeted Hilda's news that Vern was finally 'out of the closet'. The news spread through the village causing Vern some embarrassment. "I got up for a pee after a big booze-up on Christmas Day and went into the closet by mistake. I got locked in and had to stay in there until Hilda opened the door to get the Hoover out," he said today. "The thing is, what people are saying about me now is disgusting. They reckon I'm AB/CD or summat like that anyhow!"

What's Wrong with Me?

Major Seeley-Farqhar would like to know why he has always been the brunt of people's jokes and being constantly ridiculed. If you know, write to us at the usual address or telephone us at the office. The Major was said to be 'at the end of his tether'.

Reshuffle at Latecomers Club

Bob Tardy, Chairman of Cwmtwp Latecomers Club, was stripped of his office and banned from attending further meetings when it was revealed that he turned up early for their AGM on Monday.

 40

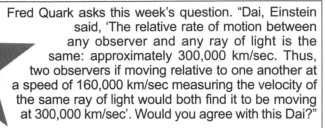

Ask Dai

Fred Quark asks this week's question. "Dai, Einstein said, 'The relative rate of motion between any observer and any ray of light is the same: approximately 300,000 km/sec. Thus, two observers if moving relative to one another at a speed of 160,000 km/sec measuring the velocity of the same ray of light would both find it to be moving at 300,000 km/sec'. Would you agree with this Dai?"

DAI SAYS: "Er… yeah."

Venice Revellers Home

The Morgans, who went to Venice for New Year are home and ready to go back to work. They have made some new friends, one of whom is a gondolier called Luigi. When covering the story, our junior reporter Tracy Tarte was heard to comment, "Gondolier? That's what the doctor said I had!"

New Word Turned Down

Cwmtwp wordsmith Alex Icon has tried to get another word introduced into the English language, this time without success. "We have many words for killing: genocide for killing a group of people, matricide for killing your mother, patricide for killing your father, fratricide for killing your brother and so on. I decided to invent a word which meant 'killing your in-laws'." A language chief said, "We cannot allow 'justified' in this context. It already exists and means something else."

Society in Trouble

The Cwmtwp Free Nelson Mandela Society is in danger of closing according to rumour. Today, its president Ronald Corrugated-Sheet said, "Interest in the society has dwindled somewhat since April 1990. We have noticed numbers dropping off for a number of years but our last AGM was a complete washout. We were pleased that Mr Mandela was released but it did herald the demise of our society to be honest. The only thing that will save us now is if they put him back inside." At the time of writing, Ron's wife Phyllis was drafting a letter to South African officials to suggest such a move.

Consumer Warning

Police have warned punters that electric fires being sold dirt cheap at Cwmtwp Market may be hot.

6

It was getting late and Nigel decided to call it a day. He had plenty to think about: the Latecomer's Club, Hell's Angles, Buzz Collins. If only he could make sense of it all!

"Open log. I'm tired. I need to sleep. I have read the events from Cwmtwp covering five months and I am still as much in the dark now as I was before the CD-ROM was found. I think I'm getting used to the language and I can make more sense of the text, although I'm unable to work out exactly what news is being reported.

"I'm beginning to have my doubts about Dai. I suspect that he may not be the fountain of all knowledge that he professes to be. Somehow, he still attracts a lot of respect from the villagers as they keep bombarding him with questions. I was not able to answer many of the questions he's been asked so far, although some of his answers were not, in my opinion, entirely satisfactory. There was a definite flaw in the answer he gave to Little Timmy Tonkin. Dai said he couldn't look directly at the sun during a solar eclipse because the moon would be in the way. This is not correct: it is to prevent eye damage. I have learned something from this mistake. It would appear that in 2005 it was only the moon that could be seen in front of the sun during a solar eclipse. I will make the Astronomers aware of this piece of information. For years, they have been trying to find out exactly when all the things floating around out there first appeared. I have all these 'things' swimming around in my head and I need to sleep. Close log."

Ten minutes later:

"Open log. Can't sleep. Lets have a look and see what more rare delights the Cwmtwp newsletter has within its pages. Let's see, June next isn't it?"

What's on in *Cwmtwp*

June

Factory Loses Contract

A Cwmtwp clothing factory has had its lucrative contract with a world-famous label withdrawn. "It was noticed that there was a very unfortunate spelling mistake on the FCUK T-shirts which was an oversight by our quality people," said Tom Oooops, MD of the factory. "Now we have a major problem in trying to shift 20,000 T-shirts with a rather strange-looking word on their fronts."

CwmtwpSPCA Drop Charges

The CwmtwpSPCA nearly prosecuted a Cwmtwp man who captured the mole that had ruined his lawn and said he was going to inflict the worst death he could think of on the animal. The CwmtwpSPCA SWAT team withdrew at the last minute with the news that the man had buried the mole alive.

Plumber Gets Cold Shoulder

Brian Froyd, a Cwmtwp man who offers a joint service of Plumbing and Philosophy, was given a bit of a cold shoulder by customer Mrs Jenkins on Thursday. After his fourth cup of tea, he sat back in a chair and asked, "Mrs Jenkins, have you ever wondered if we are all living in a big fish tank and we are merely bacteria living on the rocks in the bottom being looked over by the gods who live outside the tank?" Mrs Jenkins, who has waited four months to have her toilet fixed and was now desperate, interjected with a firm, "No, now will you please fix that pigging bog?!"

Eye Op Man Over the Moon

A Cwmtwp man who had his eyesight restored using revolutionary laser treatment has spoken of his joy at the difference it has made to his life. We joined him on a walk in the countryside – something he has not been able to do unaided for over a decade. "It's really great. I can't get over the difference it's made to my life. I wish I'd had it done years ago, it's marvellous," he said, before tripping over a sleeping cow.

Hogg Called to Hairdressers

The local police force has been called in to investigate allegations that the new ladies' hairdressers is causing some concern. Sergeant Hogg, boss of Cwmtwp Police Station who was first on the scene, was unable to see what all the fuss was about. "It seems that people have taken offence to our name," said Daphne Purm, the salon's owner. "We decided to add a bit of style by including a French term in the salon's title. I can't see anything wrong with it." The vicar added, "I don't think that 'Beau Locks' is a suitable name for a shop in this village."

Closed Pub to Re-Open

News that the long-closed pub is to re-open as a brothel has shocked residents. The vicar, who is also shocked, said, "If selling beer was unprofitable how can they make money selling soup?"

Joke Opportunity Missed

An Irishman, a Scotsman and an Englishman walked into the pub on Saturday night with an actress and a bishop. Ron Geste, leader of Cwmtwp Joke Spotters, was said to be 'on edge' when the quintet was first noticed, but his disposition changed somewhat when they had a drink and left without anything funny happening.

Man Committed

A Cwmtwp man who wanted to be a contestant on Who Wants to be a Millionaire? has been committed to Cwmtwp Asylum after putting Hilda Thicke down on the application form as his 'phone-a-friend'.

Fred's View on New Job

Fred Dinbar has told us what he thinks of his new job painting the Severn Bridge. "Actually it's a bit like painting the Forth Bridge," he said today.

Factory Bailed Out

The Chairman of the Cwmtwp Kitchen Unit Fabricators has offered to buy the T-Shirts with the spelling mistake on them. "Just the job," he said today.

£30 Break-Up

The Cwmtwp Three Tenors Tribute Band have announced that although they have lost a member due to threats from the Social, they will continue to gig as a duo and will from now on be known as '20 quid'.

Locals Try to Remember

Harold Clapper, inventor of the newt strainer and other amphibian aids, has died at his home in the USA. Harold, a Cwmtwp-born inventor, moved to the States in 1940 and became an American citizen in 1965. We went onto the streets of Cwmtwp to ask for any memories of Harold from those pre-1940 days. Bill Helter, an 86-year-old villager thought for a while and said, "Hmmm, now let me see. Clapper? Er… I can't quite place him at the moment but his name rings a bell."

Man Escapes Custody

A Cwmtwp man who has been found guilty of persistent stuttering in public has narrowly missed being sent to jail as the judge was under the impression that he would be unable to finish his sentence.

Information Announcement

Monday night's Saddo's Help Group at the Cwmtwp Community Centre has been cancelled because it clashes with Coronation Street.

Hairdressers to Merge

Staff at 'Belle Cuts' and 'Split Endz', two rival ladies' hairdressers, have decided to merge and form a new company, the new name being a combination of the old ones. Luckily, they have opted for 'Split Cuts'.

Wind of Good News

Cwmtwp has been successful in its bid to host the European Flatulence Championships in 2009. Local councillors were said to be overjoyed at the news and a spokesman said today, "We have ordered a brand new marquee and 100,000 clothes pegs which will be issued to the spectators."

Emergency at Cwmtwp Vets

An emergency situation was declared at Cwmtwp Vet's on Saturday when John Crawley, a Cwmtwp insect collector, brought in his pet centipede which was suffering from chilblains. The vet said, "This is one of the most extreme cases of animal suffering I've seen since the head keeper at Cwmtwp Zoo brought in a giraffe with a sore throat.."

Ask Dai

This week, Sam Spank, a Cwmtwp schoolboy asks, "Dai, I'm thinking of becoming a Civil Engineer. Any tips?"

DAI SAYS: "First of all, learn all about engineering. When you've done that, be very very polite to people. Servile even. All the best with your career, Sam."

Vicious Prankster?

Mrs Snodworthy, a childless woman from Shropshire, has written to us regarding a cruel joke played on her by a Cwmtwp villager. "My husband and I have tried all methods to have a baby, so far without any success. We advertised in the national press for an egg donor and the next day we received through the post half a dozen free-range from some woman called Hilda Thicke! I don't know what sort of woman she is but I must say that the prank was in very bad taste." In response to the letter, Hilda told us: "I'm a very kind woman. I saw the advert and sent the eggs straight away. Then she rang me up and went on about something called IVF and trying to have a baby. Well there's only one way to have a baby as far as I know and it certainly isn't by cadging eggs. She must think I was born under a banana boat!"

Assault in Shopping Centre

A man who was admitted to Cwmtwp Royal Infirmary was said to be recovering today after being knocked unconscious in the street on Saturday afternoon. He was treated for concussion, bruising and a few cuts. His wife said of the incident: "We were looking in this shop window and my husband said, 'that's the one I'd get' and a Cyclops ran out of the shop and hit him!"

Missed Opportunity

An office junior based in the 'Smutty Innuendo' department at Cwmtwp Joke Spotters HQ was sacked on the spot on Thursday for missing a glorious opportunity to deliver a classic line during a routine conversation. The incident occurred when a female colleague asked Timmy, the sacked worker, "Timmy, is it all right if I use your Dictaphone?" The office staff, all seeing the opportunity, waited with bated breath for his reply and were shocked when he came back with, "Aye, no problem." Timmy is to appeal on the grounds that he is not all there.

47

Oil Crisis Back On

News that oil has been found in Cwmtwp rippled through the corridors of Westminster earlier this week and several people hoped that the news may ease the Middle East situation as a source was now available in the West. A top geologist examined the sample taken from the car park at the cricket club but it was found the source was a leak from Reg Cashew's car. Reg is currently saving up for a new oil seal.

Vern Thanks AA

Vern Thicke has thanked the AA for helping him out of what was an embarrassing situation. He had locked his keys in the car and was in a bit of a panic as to how he was going to get back into it. "Luckily enough, an AA man passed in his van and I flagged him down," he said today. "I was in a bit of a spot as I couldn't get into the vehicle and my wife Hilda and dog Tiddles were locked inside."

7

It had been a tough day for Nigel and his wife. They had been discussing starting a family and had applied to Population Control at the Grand Council for a baby. They were hoping to be granted a girl, but the news had come through that morning that she would have to mother a set of male quads. This was because an incompetent stock controller at the Council had not kept an accurate record of the female offspring allocation and it was deemed that it was necessary to have a 'push' on males to those requesting children in order to bring the gender balance into equilibrium. They would also be granted a hamster for the children to interact with when they were growing up. Most of the nurturing, of course, would be undertaken by a plug-in for the thought thing which would be sent to them shortly. If they particularly wanted a girl, the department would tag one on, giving them quintuplets. They would also have to accept a concession of Panamanian Tree Frogs if they took up the parenthood offer – not for interaction with the children, but because there was a glut of them at the moment.

Another incompetent worker at the Medical Council had made a bit of a mess of Illness Allocation and Nigel had not been infected with a periodical statutory illness for quite a while. In fact, records showed that

he was overdue four bouts of minor ailments!

The incompetent worker had been reprimanded and moved into Environment to carry out the most despised job in the council: counting the parts per million in atmospheric CO_2 by hand! This was no consolation for Nigel. He had to fulfil his illness quota and would now be subjected to four minor ailments, or one major illness if he was lucky. While the major illness would not be fatal, it would satisfy the Medical Council's statistics regarding control of diseases, thus justifying the council's existence.

On a brighter note, the thought thing was working fine. The sink plug, however, was far from fine. It had been working on a 'less than efficient' basis for a few months now. Over a period of time, natural wear and tear on the plug meant that clean water left in the sink for any period of time could seep into the drainage system. This was seen as a heinous crime as these drains were designed exclusively to carry water contaminated with soap, toothpaste and excess peanut butter (you know, the layer that sticks to the roof of your mouth). If the uncontaminated water was traced back to Nigel's plughole, he could be fined the equivalent of 2.5 years' salary.

It was a truly bad day. However, the only thing that Nigel could think about was whether Mrs Jenkins had ever had her bog fixed!

What's on in *Cwmtwp*

July

Hogg Clears up Confusion

Sergeant Hogg, boss of Cwmtwp Police Station, would like to make it clear that the sign outside the station which reads 'Man Wanted for Rape' is not an advertisement and urged people to stop sending him CVs.

Compensation Worries

Bob Whatsat, a retired mineworker, is concerned that he may not get the compensation he is entitled to from the relevant authority. "I filled in the forms for Industrial Deafness and sent them off six months ago," he shouted, "and I haven't heard a thing since!"

New Directive for Fire Brigade

A crack team of fireman have been assembled at Cwmtwp Fire Station to cater for the residents of the new posh estate which has been built in the village. 'Gold Watch' as they have been nicknamed, will only serve the £250,000 luxury houses and have been told to leave a card at all call-outs asking, "Who recommended us?"

Tearaway on Trouble

Cwmtwp tearaway, Timmy Klonk, is in trouble with the local Police following reports that he had eaten an 'After Eight' mint at half past seven.

War Against Graffiti

The Mayor of Cwmtwp has urged all residents who object to graffiti in the village to sign a partition.

Lifestyle Blamed for Poverty

Eighty-year-old Flossie Grun, a spinster of Cwmtwp who had mothered and brought up thirteen children, blamed her situation on her very naïve upbringing. She told us about her life and how she had become mother to so many children. "Oh, I had a really rough time of it you know. Being an unmarried mother in those days was a terrible thing, different to today of course. I'd put it down to a very sheltered life. The first time was an air raid shelter, the second was a bus shelter… "

Ask Dai

Bill Poster, a Cwmtwp painter and decorator asks, "Dai, this has happened to me so many times and I want to know what to do the next time it happens. I put thinners in my paint when it is not runny enough, but sometimes I put too much in. Is there anything I can put in the paint when this happens? I hope you can help Dai, it will save me a fortune."

DAI SAYS: "Fatters?"

Rob Pozidrive, a Cwmtwp snout warbler, asks, "Dai, they say that the average man has a vocabulary of about 20,000 words. What do you reckon, as a man of great integrity and wisdom, is the extent of your vocabulary?"

DAI SAYS: "What's a 'vocabulary'?"

Family Stunned by Platitude

A Cwmtwp family was rendered unconscious after being cruelly subjected to an unreasonable amount of small talk, prattle and platitude on the weekend. James, the eldest son and first to regain consciousness, spoke of the ordeal today: "We had just finished lunch and my uncle, aunt and cousins called in. My aunty Mary 'small-talked' for five hours non-stop. During this time she dealt with 16,455 topics at no great depth, sometimes leaving a topic halfway through before moving on to something else totally unconnected. In the whole five hours she didn't actually say anything. She was still at it through the car window as we were waving goodbye! Most of the family passed out at some stage during the afternoon, but I think we are all on the mend now." The family have recently commissioned a medal the size of Kent to be struck for her husband, Quentin.

Triple Jump Attempt Abandoned

An attempt on the triple jump record at Cwmtwp Stadium was called off because not enough people turned up.

Bus Row

Cwmtwp Bus Company has come under fire for being 'unreasonable' following the release of the new timetable. The row concerned the rescheduling of the buses – which used to arrive in the village at two-hour intervals – with three buses all due to arrive at the same time. Mike Vindictive, boss of Cwmtwp Bus Station said, "It was Mrs Morgan's idea. She has spent the last fifteen years complaining that you waited for two hours and then three buses turned up at the same time. Well we thought we'd shut her up by making it official. I suggest that if you have any complaints you take them up with her!"

Racist Attacked

Dai Bigott, a Cwmtwp racist, is in Cwmtwp Royal Infirmary after an incident in the village on Friday night. Dai had hurled racial abuse from the window of the vehicle he was in, directed at a pedestrian who was described as being 'foreign' by eyewitnesses at the scene. The 'foreign' gentleman, who was also described as being 'very hard' by the same eyewitnesses, dragged Dai from the vehicle and beat him to within an inch of his life. Billy Helpful, chief advisor at Cwmtwp Citizens Advice Bureau said, "This is a message to all those who are in the habit of making abusive and racist comments to people of an ethnic nature: make sure that the vehicle is moving before uttering such comments and not stuck in a traffic jam at the road works outside the chip shop."

New Record at Stadium

A new UK all-comers record has been set at Cwmtwp Athletics Stadium. Ron Stayer broke the record for the long jump with a time of 3 hours 14 minutes and 8 seconds behind the North Stand after the pubs shut on Saturday night.

Rugby Seminar on Tuesday

Cwmtwp Rugby Team will attend a seminar on Tuesday night which will be conducted by an old pro who has toured with the Lions and has been in the game for 50 years. The team will receive extensive coaching on the finer points of the touring side of the game such as synchronised spewing, foul and sexist bawdy songs, drinking pints of the most vile concoctions down in one, eating equally vile concoctions in public, and a special intensive session on 'mooning' out of the back window of the bus.

Doorstep Fight

Two Avon ladies both touting for business on the same Cwmtwp estate had a fight yesterday morning in the middle of the street. Apparently, it was a right ding-dong.

Grammar Woman's Table

A Cwmtwp woman who was always bottom of the class in sentence construction in school has announced that she has bought a lovely coffee table off a woman with carved legs.

Rare Bird at Pet Shop

Cwmtwp Pet Shop has accepted a delivery of the rare Nigerian Camouflage bird. The bird, which can imitate the colour of any background, will go on sale for £29.99 as soon as the pet shop owner can find it.

53

War on Unemployment

Economists at Cwmtwp University have hatched a plan which should go a long way to solve the problem of unemployment in the village. They intend to lobby Parliament with the suggestion that the school leaving age be raised to 45.

Boring Woman Hits Back

A woman reported to have bored the people she had visited into a state of unconsciousness has hit back. She claimed it only gave one side of the story and that her conversation was very interesting. "I was not very impressed with the way you portrayed me," she said earlier today. "My conversation is absolutely riveting. Oh, that's a lovely vase. I've got one like that, only better. Where did you get it from? Oooh, I've been ill see, aye, they identify 50,000 new human diseases every day you know. Had 'em all I have, and others as well. Mind you the weather don't help. Ridiculous it is, and it'll be summer in five months! You know that woman used to live by the butchers? She's dead. Anyway lovely coffee, we have this only we get it cheaper. Supermarket we get it from, better see. You didn't tell me where you got that vase from after did you. See EastEnders last night? Awful wasn't it what she said to him. Deserved it though."

Cwmtwp Postie Criticised

A Cwmtwp postman has been severely criticised by a man who was woken up at 5am to take delivery of a snooker cue that he had bought from a mail order company. "He rang the doorbell for a good ten minutes before I got up," the disgruntled man said today. "He said he had a very long, thin thing for me and it was too wide to push through the letterbox. When I told him he could have turned it through 90 degrees and delivered the cue lengthways, he just looked at me and said, 'Oh aye'." The postman was later reported to have cancelled his appointment at the 'piles' clinic.

Steam Cleaners Sell Out

A shipment of cheap steam cleaners sold out within an hour of going on sale at Cwmtwp market on Saturday. Hilda Thicke, a satisfied customer, remarked: "Well they were cheap, but I never knew you had to clean steam!"

Ron Snigglins, a Cwmtwp elastic band stretcher, ask this week's question. "Dai, why is steel called steel?"

DAI SAYS: "Because, Ron, it's the English word for 'stahl' which is the German word for steel."

Prison Demonstration

A rooftop protest at Cwmtwp Prison was called off this morning after the chief warder reached a compromise following extensive negotiations with inmates. The convicts had complained that the prison was very cold at night and they wanted something done about it. They abandoned the protest and reoccupied their cells when prison officials agreed to put another bar on their windows.

More on Unemployment Theory

Cwmtwp Economists have added a further idea to their plan to curb unemployment. They have proposed the idea, in conjunction with the first plan, that the retirement age be dropped to 52.

Photographer Exposed

A photographer was found guilty of fraud today by a Judge at Cwmtwp Court and ordered to repay any monies obtained under false pretences. It appears that he made money by selling blank postcards entitled 'Cwmtwp Beauty Spots' to unsuspecting tourists. It has come to light that he had been trying to recoup money that he lost when he developed four films of little Ben Bunion's christening, only to find that he'd forgotten to take the lens cap off for the duration of the ceremony.

8

Meanwhile, Nigel heard there had been another major find which could rival his discovery of the Cwmtwp newsletter. It was a series of news reports from 2005 made by an organisation called ITN. Nigel did not know the format in which these stories were presented, but he did know there was a chance the new source could prove or disprove the authenticity of his Cwmtwp reports.

The person who had found the ITN reports, a Professor Roberts from a rival archaeological agency, had contacted Nigel to ask how the Cwmtwp news mongers had reported big news stories of the day. According to ITN there had been a tsunami in late December 2004 which had been widely reported in January 2005. Despite the magnitude of this event and the huge media coverage it had attracted, Nigel was bewildered by the fact that the Cwmtwp newsletter had not mentioned it at all. According to ITN and Prof Roberts, the Earth had been subjected to another natural disaster in 2005: a hurricane called 'Katrina' had devastated parts of what was then the United States of America. 'What's on in Cwmtwp' had so far made no reference to this either.

"Open log. I am very concerned about Roberts' alternative news source from 2005. Although the two sources cover the same period there is very little parity between them. The legendary tsunami was reported by ITN, so why isn't it mentioned in the newsletter? Roberts talks of hurricane Katrina and of a bomb in London which was an act of terrorism. No mention of either in my source. Roberts also talks of a huge event called 'Live 8' which actually proves the existence of music at this time. It was a collaboration between people who made music, watched by millions. Again, the compilers of 'What's on in Cwmtwp' have chosen to ignore this. Perhaps these events occurred after July. Roberts would not give me dates for these as he is very protective of his discovery. He is pushing me for information on the major events as reported in my source. I have nothing to report so far. I hope this does not degenerate into a mud-slinging match where we both try to discredit each other's work. When I look at the information I have and compare it with the amount of information that Roberts has passed on to me, I fear he may win any battle that ensues. I must try to put him off until I have found something worthwhile to tell him. Close log."

"Open communications. Professor Roberts, I have received your message and I will reply to your request soon. As you can appreciate, I have a lot of information to collate and this is taking time. Most of it is difficult to interpret and I would not like to give you any information that may be inaccurate as a result of a rushed analysis of the text. I will, therefore, delay my response until I am confident that the information I pass on to you is an accurate reflection of the events recorded in Cwmtwp in 2005. Best regards, Nigel Jones. End communications."

Nigel hoped that the news from August 2005 would give him something that he could pass on to Roberts, and shed some light on 'goings on' in the world outside Cwmtwp.

David Jandrell

What's on in *Cwmtwp*

Man Takes Club to Court

A Cwmtwp man is considering writing to someone to complain about having his application for a job turned down. "I was perfect for the job," he said today. "I have all the qualifications needed and I have years of experience. It's just not fair." In response to this claim Ron Eyebrow, secretary of Cwmtwp Lispers Club said, "You think we'd want someone with a name like Cecil St John Snetterton-Smythe Snr as our chairman? You're having a laugh."

Diarrhoea Epidemic

News spread through the village yesterday that the diarrhoea epidemic was still at its height when it was announced that 20 cases of it were brought into Cwmtwp Royal Infirmary on Friday. On hearing the news, Bill Screwdriver-Set, a long-term patient on the geriatric ward was heard to say, "Let's hope it'll taste better than the lemonade we've been having lately."

Smelling Salts Theft

A vehicle parked up overnight in Cwmtwp lay-by was stolen on Tuesday night together with its load of smelling salts. Sergeant Hogg, boss of Cwmtwp Police Station said, "Many people regard this is as a trivial offence and think its funny. Let me assure you all, it's nothing to be sniffed at!"

Rock Star Punched by Fan

Izzy Iguana, a Cwmtwp rock star who is renowned for hard drinking and debauchery, was punched in the face today by a fan who asked him for an autograph. The fan was subjected to a barrage of abuse and expletives before Izzy refused to sign his autograph book. The fan spoke of the incident saying, "I've always been a fan of Izzy and his music, but the way he treated me was disgusting. I just thought he deserved a good slap. I don't regret doing it at all." Law experts have scoured legal texts going back over 500 years and have announced that this is likely to be the first ever incidence of a case of 'a fan hitting the shit'.

Ad Man Visits Sick Aunt

Greg Satchy, chairman of Cwmtwp Institute of Advertisers, has returned home after going to see his aunt who has been ill for many years. Doctors think that she should have improved considerably, but it seems that she has more or less stayed in the same state. Greg spoke to us by telephone today about the strange condition of his Aunt Marge, saying, "I just can't believe she's not better."

Ask Dai

Tommy Tumplins asks: "Dai, I have to write an essay for my homework on quantum physics. Can you help?"

DAI SAYS: "Can't stop now Tommy, there's someone at the door!"

Marathon Called Off

Organisers of Cwmtwp Marathon abandoned the start of the race on Sunday due to a distance problem. "The problem with the distance is that we don't have enough of it," said Ron Dapper, chairman of Cwmtwp Marathon Club. "We measured up just before we were about to start and according to our ruler we're OK on the 385 yards bit, it's the other 26 miles that we have a shortage of." The competitors were sent home with a promise that it will be sorted out by next year.

Man Loses £230 in Wash

A Cwmtwp man lost his wages amounting to £230 when he left his pay packet in his trousers and his wife washed them without checking. "I was devastated," the man said today. "I knew I'd left my pay in my trousers and I panicked when I saw them hanging on the line. I rushed out and checked but it was too late – my pay was just a lump of papier mache." Sergeant Hogg, boss of Cwmtwp Police Station, has arrested the woman on a charge of money laundering.

Jailed Mum Hits Out

A woman who was released from Cwmtwp Prison just three months into a six month sentence for not sending her children to school has hit back at the authorities. "Six months should mean six months, not three! I'd just made some new friends and I was getting to be quite good at table tennis, and the next thing I know, I'm back home with these brats. Anyway, I'm thinking of making an appeal so I can finish the sentence and get through to the final of the pool competition."

Hilda Suffers Serious Burns

Hilda Thicke was admitted to the burns unit at Cwmtwp Royal Infirmary yesterday after having experienced severe burns to her feet. The consultant said that the problem would not be long term and she was allowed to go home this morning. He said that in 40 years of consulting he had never come across injuries of this nature and was at a loss as to how they could have been caused. Hilda was able to explain that she'd simply followed the instructions on a tin of rice pudding which stated that the user should 'remove the lid and stand in boiling water for twenty minutes'.

Sergeant Hogg Commended

Sergeant Hogg, boss of Cwmtwp Police Station, has been in the news following the arrest of a man walking along the High Street at 8.30pm on Thursday night. "He was dressed in slacks, had a black and white hooped T-shirt, a face mask and was carrying a large sack over his shoulder with the word 'swag' written on it. Immediately, my officers became suspicious and pulled him in." Chief Inspector Williams, Sgt Hogg's boss, said, "Whilst I commend the vigilance of the local force, I was actually on my way to a fancy dress ball at the time, dressed as a burglar. I did explain this to them but they took no notice." At the time of the arrest, Hogg stated: "A likely story. Take him into the cells, Constable and give him a sound beating." Williams stated that he was keen to talk to Hogg as soon as he was released from hospital. Sergeant Hogg had nothing to say about the matter today whilst driving away from the village in a very fast car.

Van Driver Infected

A delivery man with an unnatural affinity for the antenna on his vehicle was diagnosed with a case of Van Aerial Disease by doctors at the Cwmtwp Institute for Car Fetishists yesterday.

Doctors Encounter Odd Condition

A woman who had food surgically removed from her ears at Cwmtwp surgery was said to be suffering from an eating disorder.

Medical Complaint

A patient at Cwmtwp Surgery has complained to the BMA about treatment he received last week. When he asked for something for his liver, he was sent home with 2lbs of onions.

Naked Man Exposed

Police are investigating claims made by a Cwmtwp woman that her ex-lover is naked under all his clothes. A campaigner for decency, the Reverend Goode-Evans said today, "It is a sad state of affairs that in this day and age people are walking around naked under their clothes. It's disgusting, and the frightening thing is we probably know who they are!"

Light Thrown on Massacre

A Cwmtwp historian who has spent 50 years investigating a massacre which took place in the 19th century conflict between Abercwmtwp and Cwmtwp over ploughing rights, has been able to confirm what happened on that fateful day. The Abercwmtwpians were dug into trenches along the disputed area and were trying to create a feeling of camaraderie by giving a mass rendition of 'Old MacDonald had a Farm'. The Abercwmtwpian general noticed a rather large flurry of arrows in the air coming from the Cwmtwp archers and immediately shouted "Duck!" to his troops. On hearing this, the 50,000 Abercwmtwpians stood up and sang, "With a quack quack here and a quack quack there, here a quack… "

Hilda in Arse Scare

Hilda Thicke was said by friends and associates to be in a state of utter panic on the weekend. She is very worried about arse and has applied for a 'complete isolation' grant from the council. We spoke to her today to ascertain the nature of her fears about arse. "Oooh arse. It's terrible," she said, "You gotta watch that arse y'know. Vern is beside himself over it. Steer clear of arse, awful it is. Oh aye." We spoke to the World Health Authority to see if there were any grounds for her worries. Their top doctor was not prepared to comment, but did ask; "Does this poor unfortunate woman mean SARS?"

Ask Dai

Diane Oyly, art student at Cwmtwp University asks this week's question. "Dai, we've been told that the old masters of art and painting were probably autistic. Do you agree?"

DAI SAYS: "Absolutely Diane, of that there is no doubt. I'm quite surprised, as an art student, that you needed to ask in the first place. I was also surprised that you don't know how to spell 'artistic'. What are they teaching in university these days?"

WWTBAM Cough Incident

Ex-miner Charlie Hingram has been criticised for coughing during an episode of Who Wants to be a Millionaire and has hit back at critics. "I spent 40 years down Cwmtwp pit," he said today, " I cough all the time, not just during quiz shows and I didn't even know the answer! And anyway, I don't know what all the fuss is about, I was only watching it on the telly in the pub!"

Hogg Investigates

Sergeant Hogg, boss of Cwmtwp Police Station, has been investigating a matter brought to his attention by the manager at Cwmtwp Bank. He became suspicious when large amounts of money were being withdrawn from a Mr Morgan's account several times a day. Sergeant Hogg tracked down Mr Morgan and it transpired that his credit card had been stolen. When Sgt Hogg asked Mr Morgan why he hadn't reported the theft, he said, "Because whoever nicked it is spending less than my missus."

Woman in Toilet Scare

A woman who binges on chocolate to overcome bouts of depression made a slight mistake on the weekend. She bought 10lbs of laxative chocolate in error and ate the lot when she felt that the bottom had fallen out of her world. The outcome of the error was the world falling out of her bottom.

Golf Membership Refused

Bill Answerphone is disappointed at having his application to join Cwmtwp Golf Club turned down. Peter Fairway, Secretary of the club said, "We checked his application form and he put 'Fab Welder' down as his occupation. Well, we don't want any bigheads in this club!"

9

Nigel was a bit down in the dumps. He was having some serious doubts about his 'find'. The Cwmtwp newsletter didn't seem to be an accurate record of the events of 2005 and he was concerned that the discovery of the ITN source would cause him to lose all credibility amongst the archaeological fraternity.

"Open log. I have become increasingly concerned about the Cwmtwp newsletter and it's content. I was very enthusiastic when I began the research, but I fear that my enthusiasm may have clouded my judgment. Hilda Thicke and Dai are by no means the 'oracles' of the day as I first thought. In fact they are complete idiots even by the standards of the primitives who were alive at the time. I cannot believe that I was taken in by their 'words of wisdom'.

"I have been a fool to consider researching this document and I must not let this be seen by anyone else, particularly Roberts. He obviously has a genuine document from that time, one that reported the news 'as it happened'. He would love to get his hands on this and discredit me. He'll put pressure on me to let him have a look at it and offer me a look

at his ITN document as a carrot. What puzzles me is this: the newsletter is obviously not a record of actual world-shattering events, but what is it? What was its purpose? Who produced it, and for whom? I'll keep a low profile for the time being and see if I can glean anything from the remaining months to save face and hope Roberts doesn't get too demanding in his quest to see it. Close log."

Nigel passed a brief description of the newsletter and an account of his fears to the Department of Odd Stuff to see if they could shed some light on his dilemma. He then received an incoming message the Medical Council who had decided that he was to be given a bout of Hepatitis K to satisfy their disease statistics. It was one of those days. After taking in this bad news, there was another incoming message:

"Jones, this is Roberts. Get in touch."

"Bugger, bugger, bugger, bugger, bugger, bugger, bugger!"

Swearing was obviously one aspect of ancient life that hadn't died out.

What's on in *Cwmtwp*

September

CwmtwpSPCA Shocked

CwmtwpSPCA fundraisers were shocked when they called on a house in the village and noticed the occupants eating fish and chips in full view of an aquarium that was situated on the sideboard. They have reported the matter to their superiors and it is thought that charges will be brought. "I was shocked," said one official. "It was a flagrant display of a complete disregard for the feelings of the fish in that tank to see their own kind being eaten in front of their very eyes. The fish must have suffered a quite staggering amount of trauma and deep psychological damage." In an act of support for the CwmtwpSPCA, Sgt Hogg has placed a total ban on bacon sandwiches being consumed at Cwmtwp Police Station.

Hilda Unhappy with New Car

Hilda Thicke has complained to the local garage about a car that she and Vern bought last week. She spoke to our reporter about her objections to the vehicle from home yesterday.

"He sold it us out of false pretences he did. Useless it is, aye. We only bought it 'cos we thought it'd be handy for the shopping if we was very busy and couldn't spend the time to go out. We haven't bought a thing with it yet. Hasn't moved off the drive. Waste of money it is!" A spokesman from the garage answered Hilda's criticism by saying, "I know I sold the vehicle by saying it was an automatic, but you still have to be in it!"

Missing Tortoise

A tortoise has escaped from a garden in Cwmtwp and is still on the run. Malcolm, a 16-year-old family pet, has been missing for over a week and his owner Brian Clapton said that the matter was now causing concern and he feared for Malcolm's safety. "I've had him for years and it's a pity that he has decided to make a break for it when he did. He must have planned his getaway. I left the gate open and only turned my back on him for about three weeks and there he was – gone!"

Hospital's Most Infectious

A man with Diphtheria, Yellow Fever, Plague and SARS was put on a diet of kippers and pancakes yesterday. When asked if the diet was doing the patient any good, a doctor in charge of the case said, "Dunno, but it's the only meal we can slide under the door."

Film Buff Harasses Local

A Cwmtwp man has been taken to court on a charge of harassment. His victim, a Mr Bond, related the strange tale to us. "It appears this guy looked up the name Bond in the directory, came round here and said 'hiya', then left. I was a little puzzled by this and then he came round again a week later and said, 'So nice to meet you again Mr Bond'. Last Friday I was running for a bus and he appeared out of nowhere and said, 'Not so fast Mr Bond'. It was then that I rang Sgt Hogg."

When Sgt Hogg asked the man why he was harassing Mr Bond, he replied, "I just always wanted to say those things, that's all." It appears that the man, a big fan of 007 villains, has had similar contact with most of the 'Bonds' in the phone directory and has promised to turn over a new leaf.

Just to 'be on the safe side', Sgt Hogg, boss of Cwmtwp Police Station has ordered a shark infested, electrified pool for the station foyer, a laser capable of cutting people in half, and a big screen containing a map of Cwmtwp which rises from the floor and reaches the ceiling in his office at the touch of a button.

Music Shop Break-in

Cwmtwp Music Shop was burgled on Friday night and everything was taken apart from Reggae, Blues, Rap and Soul records. Police are on the lookout for someone with good taste in music.

Frog Expert Dies

It is with regret that we report the death of Gerry Scoutmaster, a frog expert at Cwmtwp Zoo. He croaked unexpectedly in his sleep on Monday night.

Career Change for Yob

Timmy Paigne, a local vandal, has had a change of heart following a visit to the school Careers teacher. He had strongly considered a career as a fireman but is now seeking another job since he found out that fireman actually go around putting fires out.

Black Magic Fears

An expert in the occult has claimed that there is an active witches' coven in Cwmtwp and that rituals are taking place on a regular basis. We went to the streets to find out what the underlying feelings about the allegations were. Hilda Thicke had this to say: "Well, I don't mind a bit of Black Magic, but on the whole I prefer Milk Tray."

Shooting at Cwmtwp Farm

A man was shot on Cwmtwp Farm on Friday night. It is thought that he was on his way to a fancy dress party in the village hall and decided to take a short cut through the field. The farmer, who had no regrets about the shooting, defended his action by saying: "I looked out of the window and I seen him walking through my field. He were dressed up as a bottle of Mint Sauce and I thought he were worrying my sheep!"

Lottery Odds Calculated

A team of experts have been called in to try to calculate the odds on winning the lottery. The team consisted of three mathematicians and Nigel Rockwell who is 'Reductionist to the Queen'. After several hours of calculating and arguing, the team finally opted for Nigel's theory that you had a 50/50 chance of winning the lottery on the basis that you either picked the right numbers or you didn't.

Ask Dai

Dai is on holiday so Timmy Timkinsonworth, our office junior, is going to have a stab at answering the question in Dai's absence. The question comes from Billy Goldtop, a student at Cwmtwp College of Further Excuses. "Dai, in which kind of rocks is coal found?"

TIMMY SAYS: "That's an easy one Billy, coal is found in sedimentary rocks that were laid down in the Carboniferous period." We hope this is OK, Billy. Normal service will be resumed next week when Dai comes back from his holidays.

Council Worker Sacked

Dai Wetwipes, a road painter, was sacked on Thursday for 'shirking' on the job. The Clerk of the Works said that on the first day of the job, Dai had painted three miles of double yellow lines through Cwmtwp, on the second day he had painted one mile, on the third day 50 yards and on the fourth day only two yards. In his defence, Dai said, "The trouble is, the farther I went, the farther I had to walk back to my tin of paint."

We have been contacted by the Ministry of Transport who have asked if we can print the following message on their behalf: "If anyone knows of anyone who may be travelling to Cwmtwp on the M1, please ring their mobile and tell them that the M1 doesn't go to Cwmtwp."

Turned Himself In

Jamie Sillie, a Cwmtwp youth, 'turned himself in' by accident when he took a pair of jeans back to the shop and said, "I only nicked these from here last week and the zip's gone already."

Hilda Number Change

Hilda Thicke would like to announce that after receiving lots of crank calls, she has gone ex-directory. Those wishing to ring her should pop round her house and she will make her new number available. If it is not convenient to call round her house, she says you can ring her new number on 661687 to get it.

Underpants War in Full Swing

Rival underpants firms have gone into full battle for the biggest niche in the market. A well-established underpants manufacturer which has always sold its pants in packs of six has had its market share pinched by a London manufacturer who has brought out a pack of seven – boasting a pair for every day of the week. Business moguls were today made aware of another company to enter the fray: 'Cwmtwp Underpants and Y-Front Incorporated' which has produced a pack of twelve. We asked a spokesman what their selling point was. He replied, "One for January, one for February... "

Big Lottery Winner

Burt Reynolds (no relation), a builder from Cwmtwp who won last week's Lotto Jackpot, has ordered a JCB GT to celebrate his win. The vehicle will have a plush white leather seat, a CD player and a cigarette lighter. The cigarette lighter is a young lad on a 'work experience' scheme and Burt will allow him to live in the scoop at the back of the vehicle. If he is any good and Burt decides to take him on full-time, he can move into the cab. "Something for the lad to set his sights on," said Burt this morning.

68

Man Refused Application

George Clumper, a Cwmtwp vole rattler, has had his request to join the Cwmtwp Exaggerators Club turned down once again. He told us today of his disappointment at not being allowed to join. "I must have applied 16 million times to join this club and I have not had one response to my letters." Chairman of the club, Bob Quink said in retaliation, "Not had a reply? I have written to him at least 27 million times to tell him that our membership list is full."

Tribute at Accident Spot

Flowers mark the spot where a serious road accident took place at Cwmtwp junction. The junction is between the Cwmtwp main road and the road out of Cwmtwp and is very busy, particularly on the 'going out' bit. Bill Prole and his son were injured in the crash. Bill spoke to us today from his hospital bed. "We approached the junction and I stopped. Just as I was pulling out, my son distracted my attention by saying, 'Look at all those bunches of flowers on the pavement Dad', and I pulled out right into the path of a articulated steamroller."

Village Shop Missing

Police have announced that the village paper shop has blown away.

Ask Dai

This question comes from Tom Blunt, a Cwmtwp Plank Intensifier. "Dai, I've been keeping an eye on your column and you haven't known the answer to one question since it's been going! What exactly do you know?"

DAI SAYS: "I don't know what you're on about mate."

This question was phoned into Dai's office from Ron Quietly, a Cwmtwp window-cleaner who is being treated for a rare illness. "Dai, I have a rare illness which means that my voice gets quieter and quieter the longer my sentences get. Can you give me any advice on how to get my voice back to normal?"

DAI SAYS: "Sorry Ron, I only caught half of that."

10

Nigel was feeling a little bit better. He hadn't responded to Roberts' message – with good reason. As we all know, Hepatitis K is highly contagious and transferable over the messaging system. As a result, all Nigel's outgoing messages were blocked. The Medical Council had informed all of his contacts so Nigel didn't have to worry about Roberts for the time being. Hepatitis K didn't affect incoming messages though, and the Department of Odd Stuff had informed Nigel that after having considered all the evidence, it seemed that the Cwmtwp newsletter was a good example of a 'wind up'. Nigel had a limited knowledge of linguistics, but he did know that the term 'wind up' had five meanings:

1. An action concerned with a mechanical device that used to measure time.
2. Frighten someone (as in 'put the wind up').
3. Bring something to an end.
4. Irritate someone or increase their stress level.
5. Play a prank on someone.

As far as the drivel of the Cwmtwp newsletter was concerned, Nigel felt that he could rule out the first four meanings and opt straightaway for the fifth: someone was playing a prank. He also noticed that three of the other meanings were poignant to him: Roberts was certainly putting the wind up him, and as far as winding up or bringing something to an end, his career was surely in the frame for that. Needless to say, the newsletter was beginning to irritate him intensely and his stress level had increased out of all proportion! Damned newsletter.

"Open log. My fears have materialised right in front of me. The newsletter is a fraud and I have fallen for it hook, line and sinker. There are snippets of truth buried in the reams of rubbish, but on the whole it has no historical value at all. I will read it from now on with a completely open mind. I will 'come clean' with Roberts and tell him it was a hoax – perhaps I will maintain my credibility in archaeological circles if I am open about it. Close log."

He thought that would probably be the best strategy to use – and the thought thing agreed with him. He also thought that he would make an effort to remember the real name of the thought thing as it was probably inappropriate to refer to it in such an impersonal way. The thought thing was so impressed with this that a cup of tea appeared on Nigel's desk. Nigel thought that the thought thing could also predict the future as he was about to think of a cup of tea. The thought thing sent him a message: "I knew you were going to think that." Yet another wind up.

What's on in *Cwmtwp*

October

Hogg Puts His Foot Down

Sergeant Hogg, boss of Cwmtwp Police Station, has issued a statement to all members of the public following the accident last month involving Mr Prole and his son: "I must appeal to the people of this village to stop leaving bunches of flowers by the side of the road or tied to railings. They cause accidents! I have done a survey and I've discovered that a serious road accident has always occurred right next to where people have left these flowers. It's just not on."

Cwmtwp Triangle Mystery

Experts in the paranormal have been partaking in an in-depth study of the so-called 'Cwmtwp Triangle'. Cwmtwp wives have reported mysterious disappearances of their husbands, sometimes for days on end. The experts examined the areas where the men were going missing and plotted them on the map of the village. When joined, a triangle was formed, the three points being the pub, the betting shop and the chip shop. A spokesman said, "It is safe to say that these men get caught up in this triangle and find it very difficult to get out." A spokesperson for the wives responded: "I'll give him bloomin' Cwmtwp Triangle when he gets home!"

Double Header

A chicken hatched at Cwmtwp chicken hatchery last week was found to have two heads. A scientist from the Ministry of Food, Dirt, Agriculture, Fisheries, Frog Hunting, Glue, and Sprout Warbling said, "This is most unusual."

Goldfish Dead!

Huw Jardon's goldfish Bismarck was found dead on arrival at the Vet's surgery on Thursday. "Bismarck was looking a bit peaky, so I thought I'd pop him down the Vet's for a check up," he said today. "I meant to take him down in a saucepan of water, but I grabbed a colander instead by mistake." The Vet said, "Whilst I can't tell what Bismarck had wrong with him initially, I can state that his death was down to a complete lack of water.

Competition Results

Congratulations to Mrs G Morgan of Cwmtwp who won our 'pet photo' contest with a charming snap of her tabby kitten, Snookums. She wins a brand new Gibson Les Paul guitar with gig bag and lead. "I was over the moon with the prize," she said on Tuesday. "I was 78 on Friday and it was an extra present. I've always used Fenders in the past, I've got a Strat and a Telecaster but I've never really used Gibsons. To win one was marvellous, and what a tone on it! The treble cuts you in half at high volume. It takes the varnish off the door if I really crank it up. I'll give you some more feedback on it next week."

Lifetime Ambition Achieved

Jeremy Tolpuddle has achieved his life's ambition, he announced today. "I have always looked up to people like Einstein and Newton and what they did – they changed the world really. I always wished I could do something that would never be forgotten and be talked about for ever and ever. Well I did it: I forgot our wedding anniversary," he said in casualty today, whilst awaiting treatment.

Good News for Boozers

A top professor has announced a major breakthrough in hangover research which should herald good news for hangover sufferers. "I've always found that the best thing for a hangover on a Sunday morning is to go out on the Saturday night and get really really drunk," he said today from his private room at Cwmtwp Asylum.

Ask Dai

Nigel Swott, a student at Cwmtwp University asks this week's question. "Dai, I am trying to study for my finals this week and I'm having trouble concentrating. The thing is, I live in a very noisy part of the village. I am virtually next door to the airport so I have air traffic noise all day and most of the night. I also have noisy neighbours above and below me. They play Hi-Fi's all the time. I've tried to compete but their Hi-Fi's are much more powerful than mine. Any ideas on how I can get some quiet in order to get studying done?"

DAI SAYS: "I suppose you could utilise the Hi-Fi you mentioned. Try putting your headphones on and putting a blank tape in the cassette player and playing it at full blast."

David Jandrell

Super-Hero Seeks Position

Peter Stribbling, mild-mannered Cwmtwp Super-Hero, has looked overseas in order to find an outlet for his super powers as he has not found any lucrative 'jobs' in the Cwmtwp area. Peter, who as a child was locked up in a broom cupboard by mistake, survived on household detergents and scraps found in a dust pan until he was found six weeks later. Later he developed super-human powers and under periods of great stress personifies his alter-ego and becomes Sweeperman.

"There hasn't been much interest in my super-powers so far, so I've been in touch with a few super-heroes in the States to see if there are any openings over there," he said from his secret location under his mother's sink unit. "I am able to start anytime after the 19th of next month. I have promised to give Mrs Jenkins's floor a bit of a going over in time for their daughter's party, but after that I'm free to go to the States if they need me."

We spoke to long-established hero Superman by telephone this afternoon to see if there were any opportunities for Peter, and he issued this statement: "Where did you get this number from?"

Bell-Ringer's Recruitment Drive

Anyone wishing to join the Cwmtwp Campanologist's Club should give them a bell before Friday.

Roger's Gut Problems

Roger Gormay, a Cwmtwp food enthusiast, travelled to the Middle East to sample the cuisine of the regions of the area and ended up with the Shi'ites.

Worker Loses Fingers

Bill Prittstick took so many Aspirins before going to work on Saturday morning, he didn't notice when he cut off his index and middle fingers off his right hand at the Cwmtwp Saw Mill. "I had a hangover after winning the tote on Friday night. I took about a dozen tablets and didn't notice I'd lost the fingers until I went to wave goodbye to the boss," he said.

University Degree Awarded

We would like to congratulate Mrs Jenkins of Croupe Avenue, Cwmtwp for an outstanding educational feat. At the age of 58 she has passed an honours degree in watching the telly at six o'clock in the morning.

Eisteddfod Winner

Congratulations to Megan Jones (aged 6) of Cwmtwp who won the chair for the Dirty Poem Contest at the Cwmtwp Royal Welsh Eisteddfod last Saturday. Unfortunately, the poem is unprintable and has been omitted from this report on legal advice. Sources close to Megan said, "It's an absolute corker!"

Anniversary Disaster

Vern and Hilda Thicke's anniversary plans did not go very smoothly according to gossip going round the village today. They decided to celebrate by going to the cinema. They spent 13 hours standing outside the Cwmtwp Odeon waiting to go in to watch a film that they believed was called Closed for Refurbishment. They were later ejected from the 24-hour Vegan restaurant for ordering steak and chips.

Cracker Called in

A Police 'cracker' psychologist has been brought in to build a profile of persons who have been committing heinous crimes in the area. The village has been subjected to a series of car thefts, muggings and acts of violence. After serious studies of all the crimes that have occurred, the psychologist was in a position to issue this statement: "It is my belief that the person or persons responsible for these acts may well be up to no good."

Thief Apprehended

A Cwmtwp man was held in custody after being stopped in the street by an off-duty officer who suspected that the man was in illegal possession of a very large sign saying 'LONG VEHICLE.' The only excuse that the man was able to offer for having the sign was that it had fallen off the back of a lorry.

Trials for New Players

The trials for new players took place at Cwmtwp Rovers on Thursday night. As only eleven players were available for the session, manager Ron Sprig placed eleven dustbins at random around the pitch so that the players could dribble around them in a mock game. The game was abandoned after 20 minutes as the dustbins were winning 4-0.

New Shop For Village

A new shop is to open in the village selling Bonsai trees. Tim Querqus, a Cwmtwp tree enthusiast, has always been very interested in growing Bonsai trees and decided to combine his interest with a means of making a living. "I planted the seeds last weekend to start the trees growing," he said. "I imagine the first trees will be ready to go on the shelves in about 76 years time."

Congratulations!

A Cwmtwp woman who craved eating elastic bands throughout her pregnancy was admitted to Cwmtwp Maternity Ward at Cwmtwp Royal Infirmary late last night. After a short period of labour she gave birth to a bouncing baby girl at 7.15, 8.35, 9.10, 9.35, 10.10, 11.02 and 11.55 this morning.

Anorexia Club Fracas

There was trouble at the Cwmtwp Anorexia Club's AGM last night. Members were talking about how they were going to celebrate the 10th anniversary of the club's existence, when one suggested going out for a meal. He was forcibly removed from the club by the other members.

Dinnerlady Honoured

Gladys Viking, dinnerlady at Cwmtwp Community Centre, has been honoured for her long service. She was presented with a gold watch after 30 years slaving over a hot stove to feed the villagers with top quality food. She enjoyed the presentation and for once, tucked into food at the Community Centre that had been prepared by someone else. When she got home, her husband Basil had this to say about her 30 years in the kitchen: "Where the hell have you been?"

Thicke Family in Torment

The Thicke family was rocked by news that a relative from Cardiff has announced that their son has recently qualified as a barrister. Hilda, in shock, spoke out. "We were all hoping some good would come of this lad, he was always very bright and good in school. Now we've found out he spent over seven years in college only to end up as a handrail on the top of the stairs!"

11

Nigel had followed his own advice and read the October issue with an open mind. He didn't expect anything from it; he didn't look too deeply into the words and try to find something that wasn't there. Bearing this in mind, his attitude was beginning to change. It was like a breath of fresh air! What fantastic real life stories!

"Open log. I have begun to see the Cwmtwp newsletter in a completely different light. Throughout my whole life I have been reading texts and studying ancient artefacts to try to 'find the truth' about momentous events in history – and for what? There's just as much value in finding out about ordinary people's lives. Roberts can carry on with his quest to satisfy his thirst for knowledge of important events; that's not for me anymore. I shall give him the newsletter and I don't care what he thinks.

"I think the newsletter still has value as a historical document even if it doesn't mention the main news stories of the day. After all, how much of the history and archaeology that we teach these days is a 100% accurate account of

events? My guess is none of it. And let's face it: many of the historical tomes we have produced have been based on conjecture. In many cases gaps in our knowledge have been filled by guesswork because the information we had was incomplete or untranslatable.

"The Department of Odd Stuff labelled the newsletter a 'wind up', but this was based on a very sketchy outline of the content I gave them. I, on the other hand, have read every word and have come to know these people. I know what made them tick, I know the way they thought, I know how they dealt with situations. This is real life. They lived in their own little world where nothing else mattered outside the boundaries of the village. They weren't concerned about tsunamis and Live 8 and world-shattering events. However, if someone went to the pub with a new pair of socks on a Friday night, everyone in the village would know about it by 10 o'clock the following morning. These are the things which mattered. It was 'news' and thankfully someone recorded it all. Close log."

Nigel thought about a cheese and onion sandwich and an orange juice. Nothing happened. He thought about them again. Still nothing. He looked at the thought thing and saw it was facing the other way. He thought that maybe it was sulking because he had intended to refer to it by its proper name but hadn't bothered. He was right!

Hilda's Bonfire Party Off!

The Thickes have called off their bonfire party because they are very wary of the instructions printed on the fireworks. Hilda apologised to all the guests and added, "You can't be too careful with these firework things you know. They go off see! Well, I was reading the instructions and they said 'Light Blue Touch Paper and Retire'. Well, the touch paper is dark blue and I'm only 47!"

Angling Success

Cwmtwp Fishing Club organised a competition on the weekend which was a great success. Entrants were only allowed to fish from the bridge, but despite the restrictions many fish were caught, some of a record size. The best catches were a 56lb pike, a 32lb trout and a 112lb carp. A special mention must go to Bob Rifleman who fished off the railway bridge by mistake and caught the 3.15 to Paddington using only maggot and worm. Bob is currently in a competition fishing the Thames, trying to win enough money to get back home.

Uncouth Darts Final

Cwmtwp Belch-the-Alphabet Club have lost the final of the Uncouth Darts Clubs tournament to Abercwmtwp Nosepickers 'A' Side. The Captain of the Cwmtwp team, Ron Colic, who can belch the alphabet in 47 seconds, spoke to us after the game. "It is a pity that they have beaten us once again. In the five years that the Uncouth Darts Clubs League has been in existence, we have never been victorious against them. I was hoping we would make it for the first time tonight and lift the trophy. I suppose it's fair to say that the Abercwmtwp Nosepickers are our bogey side."

Garage's New Method

Cwmtwp Repair Garage will test all foreign vehicles with a new piece of equipment consisting of a duck with a spring attached to each wing and foot. A spokesman for the garage said, "The technology is German and is known as the 'four spring duck technique'."

Cwmtwp City of Culture?

The result of the 'City of Culture' bid has disappointed local dignitaries. Cwmtwp came last in the poll of 2,357 cities worldwide, 57 votes behind the last-but-one bid, a pile of broken glass 70 miles north of Beirut.

Duo Done By Tax Office

Cwmtwp Tax Officials have had a success with their latest investigation. They had a music duo under surveillance as they suspected they may not be declaring their earnings to them. It was revealed that the guitarist was acting according to the law and was regularly making payments. However, the second member of the duo, John Bower, the bloke that plays the violin, has been done for fiddling.

Should've Seen it Coming

Extrovert Bob Loude came a cropper today. He climbed the statue of Bill Pryce-Cutt, an 18th century Cwmtwp statesman and tried to balance on the bridge of the nose whilst holding two pieces of circular glass. Bob fell from the 320-foot high statue and was taken to Cwmtwp Hospital for treatment. His wife Jayne said, "I told him not to go up that statue and make a spectacle of himself." She was later arrested by Sgt Hogg for being in breach of new pun laws.

Hilda in Grill Confusion

Hilda Thicke was so impressed with the advert for the George Foreman Lean Mean Grilling Machine that she decided to buy one. Unfortunately, when she asked for the item at the shopping precinct she got slightly muddled up and asked for, "One of them George Formby things please." What made matters worse was the fact that she had gone into Cwmtwp Music Shop by mistake. She was last seen bouncing two burgers and half a dozen sausages up and down on a £300 ukulele banjo.

Vet Bill Queried

Ron Fiscal, a Cwmtwp dog owner, has queried a vet bill that he was given after taking his dog to the local surgery. "I took Rover in to see the vet and he told me he was dead. I asked for a second opinion and he brought in this Labrador. The Labrador sniffed Rover and barked and the vet said that the Labrador had agreed that Rover was dead. I was not satisfied with this and the vet brought in a Siamese who pawed Rover and then purred. The vet said that the moggy agreed that Rover was dead and charged me £50! Extortionate!" The vet responded: "If this bloke had listened to me the bill would have been £10, but he insisted on the lab test and the cat scan."

Man in Hiding in Bogs

A man wanted by the Police was seen entering a cubicle in Cwmtwp toilets in the High Street on Friday afternoon. Police were called and were on the scene in minutes. Sergeant Hogg, boss of Cwmtwp Police Station said, "We're going to give it ten minutes before we go in."

Serious Diarrhoea Strain

A Cwmtwp man who is suffering from a very aggressive form of sudden diarrhoea attacks has been told it is of the hereditary diarrhoea type. When he asked what that was, doctors said, "It's in your genes!"

Daffodil Sandwiches!

Fred Grimbles, a Cwmtwp snod woobler, was admitted to Cwmtwp Royal Infirmary yesterday after a mix-up in the kitchen. After a few pints in the pub he fancied some cheese and onion sandwiches. He was slightly 'the worse for wear' and used daffodil bulbs instead of onions. He became very ill and was taken into hospital for a routine check. Doctors decided to keep him in and said that he should be out in the Spring.

Double Wedding Planned

A double wedding is to take place in the village soon. Twins Donna and Sheesh Kebab are to marry their boyfriends Egon Toast and Terry Marsalata in an eagerly awaited ceremony at the Chapel as soon as the priest, Pastor Sauce, can fit them in. Villagers are said to be very interested to see what food will be served at the reception.

Tom Loses Girlfriends

Tom Fitbloke, Cwmtwp user and abuser of women, was perturbed to find that all his girlfriends had found out about each other and had systematically finished with him. "I went from having six girlfriends to none at all in the space of two days," he said today.

He was consoled by his best mate Ron who said, "Never mind Tom, your girlfriends are like buses." Tom replied smugly, "You mean there'll be another one along in a minute?"

To which Ron said, "No Tom, I mean your girlfriends are like buses!"

Serial Lover in Hospital

A man was admitted to Cwmtwp Royal Infirmary last week and found to be suffering from Aids, Syphilis, Gonorrhoea, Crabs and Chlamydia. Today, doctors described the man as being an 'incurable romantic'.

Double Trouble

Hilda Thicke is back from her holidays with a few problems. She has acute abdominal pains and serious sunburn problems. She said today, "Well, that coconut suntan stuff was useless. I've never ever tasted anything quite as bad as that."

Doorman Course Shelved

A course that was planned to take place in Cwmtwp Community Centre was called off at the last minute. The course was to train doormen in the art of 'bouncing' at the Cwmtwp 'nightspots' which can become pretty rowdy at times. The course was called off when Ron Rockhard, a bouncer of 30 years who was going to teach the group, didn't gain entry to the classroom because he turned up without a tie on.

Mixed Feelings

Rugby fan Jon Propp was over the moon after winning an internet auction for a Rugby World Cup Final jersey that had been signed by both teams in mud from the pitch. It was later revealed that he was 'less over the moon' when he got home from work yesterday to find that his mother had washed and ironed it.

Archaeological Find

Archaeologists from the four corners of the earth flew into the village yesterday to examine some 'stones' that had appeared on some waste ground outside the village. A top archaeologist spoke of the find, saying, "This could be a very important find. The stones appear to be building material and their apparent appearance out of thin air may indicate a connection with the occult." However, the mystery was quickly solved when a big white van arrived and two men used the stones to start building a wall.

Part-Time Job for Retired Farmer

Retired farmer Bob Silage who was a great lover of tractors, but doesn't like them anymore, has got a job at Cwmtwp Pungent Gas Factory as an extractor fan.

Pleased with New Car

Ian Forestofdean has bought a new diesel car. "What swayed me," he said, "was when I asked the man in the garage if it used much petrol, he said it didn't use any at all!"

Ask Dai

Dave Doozly, a Cwmtwp bird enthusiast asks, "Dai, I have a cockatiel and I haven't given it a name yet because I don't know if it's male or female. Do you know how to tell the sex of cockatiels?"

DAI SAYS: "Easy mate. Just give it some seeds and if he eats them it's a male and if she eats them it's a female."

12

The thought thing had started behaving itself again. This is probably because Nigel thought of getting a new one when it began to sulk.

Nigel was interested to see what Roberts would say about the newsletter. He had refused Roberts' offer to view his ITN source. Apparently it was completely factual and even contained 'footage'. But Nigel did not want to know what the Houses of Parliament looked like or hear Tony Blair's voice for real or watch highlights of the FA Cup final (whatever that was). What he really wanted was to be able to walk through Cwmtwp village in the year 2005, eat a buffet supplied by 'Ocksboll', see what courses were on offer at Cwmtwp College of Further Excuses, experience Ballykiss-soddin-angel first-hand and join Cwmtwp Belch-the-Alphabet Club. Most of all he wanted to fall foul of the law and experience the attentions of the intrepid Sergeant Hogg. What was he like? He was always referred to as 'boss of Cwmtwp Police Station'. Did he insist on this phrase being added to any reference to his name? If only he could go back and meet him in person.

"Open log. I have been thinking about the characters in the newsletter a lot lately. As I have been reading the stories

I have built up a mental picture of the people who lived there in 2005. There are three very prominent characters who dominated the news. Whoever penned this newsletter seemed to think that what these three did warranted regular reporting.

"Sergeant Hogg – what a character! Obviously a large chap as he always seemed to be involved in food-related activities. He didn't tend to make statements from the Police Station but from the chip shop or the cake shop. He seemed to use his position to make his own life easier. He was never actually there when these 'heinous crimes' took place, but always had a lot to say about them when he finally arrived at the scene. And what he said was never much of a help; in most cases it made things worse!

"Dai is a bit of a mystery. His surname is never printed. I wonder who he was. He had a regular column in the newsletter as 'resident expert'. The truth of the matter is, he didn't know the answer to anything! When faced with a question that floored him he would fob off the readers with a pathetic smokescreen – and the most surprising thing was, they worked. The questions kept coming, and he kept fobbing them off. Did the locals realise this or did they really think he was the guru he portrayed himself as?

"Hilda, bless her. She didn't really know what was going on did she? She got herself into some terrible scrapes, usually as a result of misunderstanding the situation she was in. What a marvellous woman. Naïve and uncomplicated, but she survived. Took everything in her stride. I actually fancy Hilda. The mental picture I have of her is of an attractive woman and I think she may have had a few secret admirers in Cwmtwp. Close log."

The thought thing looked at Nigel's mental picture of Hilda and agreed that she was a bit on the smart side.

David Jandrell

Shoppers Given a Treat

Shoppers at the precinct were given a rare treat today when the Cwmtwp Salvation Army Silver Punk Band performed festive songs for them. They gave a tremendous rendition of 'Anarchy in the UK' followed by a medley of Punk classics from the late '70s and early '80s. To show their versatility they finished off with a cover of The Who's 'My Generation' which culminated in an instrument smashing scene, the likes of which has never been witnessed in the precinct. The antics of Mankin' Marjory, the band's tambourinist, were described as 'vile' by onlookers.

Thickes in Hospital

The Thickes are all in the food poisoning ward at Cwmtwp Royal Infirmary after their Christmas dinner. Hilda spoke of the event from under the door in the toilet block. "I was told you had to cook the turkey for 20 minutes a pound and an extra 20 minutes. Well our turkey only cost me a fiver as I was in the 'Christmas Club' in the butchers. So I cooked it for two hours and now look at us! Once again we have been the victims of unclear instructions. I think there ought to be a law against it."

Suitor gets it Wrong

A man who approached a woman in a pub and presented her with a homemade beehive was sent away with his 'tail between his legs' it was reported today. The woman snubbed his advances and he was reportedly 'very upset'. He had fancied the woman for a long time. His friend who was experienced in wooing ladies had given him some advice but it appeared he had misheard the suggestion to 'make a beeline for her'.

Dress Up Warm

The Cwmtwp Society for Using Words that Sound the Same but are Spelt Different and Amateur Meteorologists have warned that we are in for a bad spell of whether.

Nit Cure Investigated

Nigel Noobler, a Cwmtwp inventor, has devised a new method of getting rid of head lice. The new method involves washing the affected head with vodka and then sprinkling it with sand. The theory behind the method is that the lice get drunk and then kill each other by throwing rocks around. Fred Quimbly, head of Parasitic Head Complaints at the Cwmtwp Institute of Crackpot Cures had this to say: "Obviously we'll need to investigate this matter more thoroughly, but at first glance it appears to be a very good idea indeed."

Hogg Issues Warning

Sergeant Hogg, boss of Cwmtwp Police Station, has issued a warning to all people who do not want to be murdered. The warning comes as a result of Hogg watching hundreds of hours of footage of the TV programme Murder She Wrote. The statement, issued by Cwmtwp Police Station read, "If you are ever in a carriage on a train or at a dinner party and that Jessica Fletcher arrives, GET OUT OF THERE!"

Ask Dai

A festive question this week from Archibald Tinsel who asks, "Dai, what are you getting for Christmas?"

DAI SAYS: "Drunk."

Ron Bunter, a pimple wedger from Cwmtwp asks, "Dai, I'm a great big fat slob. I've tried everything to lose weight apart from eating less and exercising. Any ideas?"

DAI SAYS: "Try eating what you like, just don't swallow it."

Five-Legged Woman Sorted

Doris Tabkey, Cwmtwp's only five-legged woman, has been to see a lingerie expert to discuss the problem that she has finding underwear to fit her. She spoke to us today about the problem. "Having five legs, it is hard to buy clothes to fit. Standard sizes of underwear are really uncomfortable, but ever since I had a meeting with the lingerie expert, I am much better off. I was measured and had several fittings and they have made lingerie exclusively for me. Now my knickers fit me like a glove."

Hogg in Hospital

Sergeant Hogg, boss of Cwmtwp Police Station, was admitted to Cwmtwp Royal Infirmary today. Doctors said he was being treated for an overdose of mince pies.

Stig Taken to Academy

Stig Heathen, a Cwmtwp man, has been taken away to the Cwmtwp Academy of Anthropology by an anthropologist for further study, it was revealed today. "I saw this bloke in the Rugby Club on Friday night downing buckets of Guinness and cider in one," said the expert from his laboratory which contains a glass case with Stig in it. "I recognised him as a species of Neanderthal, the likes of which were thought to be extinct for at least 30,000 years. I immediately claimed him as an area of acute scientific interest and stuck him in this case until we can decide what to do with him." The Chairman of Cwmtwp Rugby team said, "It's all very well declaring Stig an area of scientific interest, but it leaves us with the unenviable task of finding a new number 8!"

Ozzie Goes Back

An Australian man who married a Cwmtwp woman eighteen months ago has 'had a change of heart' and decided that he would prefer 'male' company. He told his wife of his decision then packed his bags and went back to Sydney.

Trouble for Amnesiacs

Police were called to an incident at the Amnesiac Society's AGM on Monday night. When asked to recall the incident, Chairman Bill Shorthand scratched his head and said, "It was like this... er... um... "

Burglar Sentenced

A burglar who broke into Cwmtwp Elastic Band Factory and stole 18,000 elastic bands was sentenced today at Cwmtwp Crown Court. Summing up, the judge said, "It's my duty to make you pay for your crime and the only option is to ensure you get a very long stretch."

Terrorism Fears

Cwmtwp Boiled Egg Factory was put on alert today following fears about the amount of terrorism in the world at the moment. To put workers' minds at rest, the Ministry of Defence has allocated 500 soldiers to the place.

Judge Contacts Law Lords

A judge at Cwmtwp Crown Court has contacted the hierarchy of the legal profession to ask advice on a particular case. He was about to pass sentence on Ron Stig Trump, Cwmtwp's worst felon and has asked the Law Lords if the term 'chuck the key away' is a legitimate legal phrase.

Hogg in Court Row

Sergeant Hogg, boss of Cwmtwp Police Station, found himself in a spot of bother with his superiors following an oversight when giving evidence in what was considered an 'open and shut' case at Cwmtwp Crown Court.

When being cross-examined, Sgt Hogg asked if he could refer to his notes and he started quite well. His evidence began with the usual parlance, "I was proceeding in an orderly fashion in a northerly direction… " but deteriorated drastically when he turned over the page and continued with, "Four pounds of spuds, a bottle of milk, a loaf of bread, biscuits and an extra-large, extra-strength tube of Anusol."

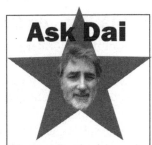

Ask Dai

Timmy Packed-Lunch, a Cwmtwp schoolboy, asks this question. "Dai, can you help me with my homework? The question is: 'What did Sir Walter Raleigh bring back to this country?'"

DAI SAYS: "That's an easy one Timmy, it was the bicycle.

Break-in at Store

Cwmtwp electrical store was broken into on the weekend and everything was taken apart from a trouser press and an iron. Police are on the lookout for anyone walking around looking crumpled.

Shop Opening Flop

Men from all over the valley were disappointed when they were allowed into the new shop that opened this morning in the High Street. The men had queued all night for the opening of 'Hoes R Us' and rushed in as soon as the doors were unlocked. A spokesman for the men said, "We've waited eagerly for this shop to open ever since they put the sign up. This morning was a great shock to us when we got inside to find the place full of gardening implements."

Zoo Keeper Missing

When Billy Primate, keeper of apes at Cwmtwp Zoo, did not come home from work last Friday, his mother assumed that he had stayed with friends. However, when it was noticed that a gorilla had also gone missing on the same day, it became apparent that they had 'run away' together. When we asked his mother if he had eloped with a male or female gorilla, she was very indignant and shocked by the question. When pressed for an answer, she said, "Female of course! There's nothing funny about our Billy!"

David Jandrell

Santa Back on Dole

R Jimlad, a former pirate on Cwmtwp Boating Lake, was today signing on again following his annual stint as Santa at The Cwmtwp Department Store. He spoke of his future to our reporter this morning. "Since giving up pirating, I have found it difficult gaining work. I do, however, get work every year in the last three weeks of December. It is regular but seasonal if you know what I mean. If only I could do a bit of pirating throughout the year just to keep my hand… er sorry, hook in."

Sgt Hogg's Disappointment

Sergeant Hogg, boss of Cwmtwp Police Station, is pondering yet another year without being included in the New Year's Honours list. "This is the 40th year on the trot I've been excluded," he said today. "And when you think of the nonsense I've had to put up with in this place, I should have been given a gold medal the size of Luton by now." Sergeant Hogg had to cut his statement off at that point as he received a 999 call to investigate a reported dispute over who was going to pull the wishbone from an Xmas turkey.

A Happy New Year to all our readers!

See you all next year

Nigel had finished reading the newsletter! A warm glow came over him as he reflected on the twelve months' worth of stories from Cwmtwp. What an experience. He sent a message to the lads who had found the CD-ROM thanking them from the bottom of his heart for passing it on. He also told them about the enormous fun he'd had as a result of their find. He was a little perturbed when they responded to his message by saying, "I bet you didn't have as much fun with that one as we had with the others." The others! What others? There were others? Oh my God!!!! He invited the lads around to ask about them.

"Tell me guys, when you gave me the CD-ROM, why didn't you mention that there were others?"

"Well, it was the only one we had at the time. But we went back to place where we found it and had a poke around and found five more. These had writing on them."

"What did the writing say?"

"2006, 2007, 2008, 2009 and 2010."

"And where are they now?"

"Dunno"

"You don't know?!"

"Well, we heard about this really ancient game called Frisbee so we played it. It involved throwing a little flat round thing as far as you can. These CD-ROM things were just the job. They went for miles. Trouble is after a couple of goes they all broke. It was great up until then though."

Nigel was devastated. Five years' worth of Cwmtwp gone forever!

"Well thank you very much for the one you gave me. It has changed my life. What are your names by the way?"

"Timmy Forestofdean, Sir Roger Rhys Jones Williams Morgan Griffiths Smythe Ponsonby Barrington Rathbone St John Speedwagon Mastercard Lewis Bicarbonate Brasenose Eel Envelope Ullricht Benson Squidgelin Les Abacus Francis Angelis Peterstone Robinson Rutle Gilmour Inkjet Walmar Dennis Tilsley Highland Spring Arcade Embassy Jenkins, Tom Hogg, Billy Seeley-Farqhar, David Tarte and Ron Thicke."

The A-Z of Welsh Rugby

Richard Rowe

Tales of drunkenness and silliness abound in this remarkable field study. The author courageously dives head-first into the rough-and-tumble of Welsh rugby to investigate such diverse aspects of the sport such as hangovers, karaoke, police stations, xenophobia, cheating referees, pranks on the team bus and heroic drinking bouts. Enjoy the sordid stories of going-away trips with behind-the-scenes insights - inadvertently showing why we are so proud to be Welsh.

£3.95
ISBN: 9780862439484

Welsh Valleys Humour

David Jandrell

A first-time visitor to the south Wales Valleys will be subjected to a language that will initially be unfamiliar to them. This book features a tongue-in-cheek guide to the curious ways in which Valleys inhabitants use English, together with anecdotes, jokes, stories depicting Valleys life, and malapropisms from real-life Valleys situations!

"What a delight David Jandrell's book is!"
– **Ronnie Barker**

£3.95
ISBN: 0 86243 736 9

Welsh Valleys Characters

David Jandrell

If you enjoyed Welsh Valleys Humour you will enjoy this picture of valleys life with portraits of the typical pub landlord, club character, builder and nosey parker. Enjoy this delightful introduction to these real characters – their haunts, habits and humour; with a special section of hilarious answers to real valleys pub quizzes!

£3.95
ISBN: 0862437725

Wenglish

Robert Lewis

Two books in one, Wenglish combines the practical qualities of a reference book with a general introduction to Wenglish, the English dialect of the South Wales Valleys. It gives the perfect introduction to how the dialect developed in the first place, and the part played by the people who speak it and the landscape itself. As a reference book it offers an alphabetical glossary, dialogue examples, grammar and exercises, so that you can try your hand or even teach yourself Wenglish, as well as learning all about it.

£9.95
ISBN: 9781847710307

This book is just one of a whole range
of Welsh-interest publications from
Y Lolfa. For a full list of books currently
in print, send now for your free copy of
our new, full colour catalogue.
Or simply surf into our website

www.ylolfa.com

for secure on-line ordering.

TALYBONT CEREDIGION CYMRU SY24 5AP
e-bost ylolfa@ylolfa.com
gwefan www.ylolfa.com
ffôn (01970) 832 304
ffacs 832 782